RESTLESS SPIRIT

"I realize more and more what it takes to be a really good photographer. You go in over your head, not just up to your neck."

—Dorothea Lange

RESTLESS SPIRIT

THE LIFE AND WORK OF DOROTHEA LANGE

by Elizabeth Partridge

VIKING

For my father, Rondal Partridge

❖   ❖   ❖

Grateful thanks to my editor, Jill Davis; my agent Ruth Cohen; the greater Dixon-Taylor-Lange clan, particularly Christina Gardner and Helen, John, and Dan Dixon; Drew Johnson, Janice Capecci, and Joy Tehan at the Oakland Museum; Beverly Brannon at the Library of Congress; Sue Bartolletti, Roger Daniels, Gary Hilander, the Frosters, Linda Glaser, and especially my sister, Meg Partridge.

VIKING
Published by the Penguin Group
Penguin Putnam Inc., 375 Hudson Street, New York, New York 10014, U.S.A.

Penguin Books Ltd, Registered Offices: Harmondsworth, Middlesex, England

First published by Viking in 1998, a member of Penguin Putnam Books for Young Readers

1   3   5   7   9   10   8   6   4   2

LIBRARY OF CONGRESS CATALOGING-IN-PUBLICATION DATA
Partridge, Elizabeth.
Restless spirit : the life and work of Dorothea Lange / by Elizabeth Partridge.
p.   cm.
Includes index.
Summary: A biography of Dorothea Lange, whose photographs of migrant workers, Japanese
American internees, and rural poverty helped bring about important social reforms.
ISBN 0-670-87888-X
1. Lange, Dorothea—Juvenile literature. 2. Women photographers—United States—Biography—
Juvenile literature. [1. Lange, Dorothea. 2. Women photographers. 3. Photographers.
4. Women—Biography.] I. Lange, Dorothea. II. Title
TR140.L3P37 1998 770'.92—dc21 [B] 98-9807 CIP AC

Printed in Singapore • Set in Bembo
Designed by Denise Cronin

DOROTHEA LANGE'S PHOTOS ARE FROM THE FOLLOWING SOURCES:

Bancroft Library, University of California, Berkeley, pages 66, 88; Still Pictures Division, National Archives, pages 82, 83, 84, 85, 86; The Dorothea Lange Collection, the Oakland Museum of California, gift of Paul S. Taylor, pages 2, 3, 4, 9, 21, 24, 28, 30, 32, 33, 34, 35, 41, 42, 43, 44, 45, 49, 53, 56, 69, 76, 79, 87, 92, 93, 94, 95, 97, 99, 100, 102, 103, 104, 108, 109, 110; Private collections, pages 11, 23, 29, 36, 47, 57, 58; U.S. Farm Security Administration, Prints and Photographs Division, Library of Congress, front and back cover, pages 51, 60, 61, 62, 67, 68, 70, 71, 72, 75, 77, 78.

IMAGES BY OTHER PHOTOGRAPHERS ARE FROM THE FOLLOWING SOURCES:

The Ansel Adams Publishing Rights Trust, page 96; Arnold Genthe Collection, Library of Congress, page 18; Brown Brothers, Sterling, Penna., pages 12, 14; Imogen Cunningham Trust, photo by Imogen Cunningham, print by Ron Partridge, page 46; Ron Partridge, all rights reserved, pages iii, vi, 26, 54, 64, 74, 106, 112, 114, 116, 117; Private collections, pages 6, 10, 16, 90; Paul S. Taylor, the Dorothea Lange Collection, the Oakland Museum of California, gift of Paul S. Taylor, page 38; U.S. Farm Security Administration, Prints and Photographs Division, Library of Congress, page 80.

Contents

Foreword
Starving Pea Pickers 1

Chapter One
Limpy 7

Chapter Two
Portrait Photographer 17

Chapter Three
Conflicting Demands 27

Chapter Four
To the Streets 39

Chapter Five
Starved, Stalled, and Stranded 47

Chapter Six
Sliding in on the Edges 55

Chapter Seven
Hardship in the Fields 65

Chapter Eight
The South 75

Chapter Nine
Japanese American Internment 81

Chapter Ten
The Shipyard Years 91

Chapter Eleven
World Travels 97

Chapter Twelve
The Right Time 107

Afterword
Thanksgiving 113

Bibliographic Note 118

Index 120

Dorothea, Berkeley, 1936 (Photograph by Ron Partridge)

STARVING PEA PICKERS

*"There are moments such as these when time stands still. All you
do is hold your breath and hope it will wait for you."*

Dorothea Lange tightened her grip on the steering wheel and peered through
the rain beating against the windshield. It was the end of a cold, miserable winter.
She had been traveling alone for a month photographing migrant farmworkers in
California. Now her camera bags were packed and she was heading home. On the
seat beside her was a box full of exposed film, ready to be mailed back to
Washington, D.C. Her time was up, and she was worked out, tired to the bone.

It was early March 1936. The Great Depression and terrible dust storms in the
Midwest had torn tens of thousands of farmers from their land. They had packed
up a few belongings and come to California, driving battered old cars or pickup
trucks, riding the rails, or tramping along the road, thumbing rides. Some came
alone, but many brought their families. They were looking for work, any kind of
work, to keep from starving. What they knew was farming, so they headed for the
rich agricultural fields of the West.

Once they made it to California they moved from county to county following
the ripening crops, earning as little as four dollars a week picking peaches, plums,
potatoes, and cotton. Homes for the migrants were old tents or cardboard boxes
and flat pieces of tin thrown together into a shelter. People washed themselves in
the same ponds and irrigation ditches they drew their drinking water from. They
went to the bathroom in wooden outhouses or they hid behind bushes.

The government had hired Dorothea to take pictures of the migrants' living
and working conditions. They worked sixteen-hour days, and so did she. She

began at sunup and photographed until the evening light faded from the fields. By the end of each day, she was worn out from the long hours and the misery she had seen. But the next morning she woke up early and began all over again.

But now Dorothea's trip was nearly over. As the miles passed, she stared out at the wet and gleaming highway stretching ahead of her. The rhythmic sound of the windshield wipers filled her with relief. Sixty-five miles an hour would get her back to her family in seven hours. Finally she could take her mind off her work and think of home.

A homemade sign flashed by—PEA PICKERS' CAMP. She didn't want to stop, and she didn't. But as she drove, she started to argue with herself.

"Dorothea, how about that camp back there?"

"To turn back certainly is not necessary. Haven't you plenty of photographs on this subject? Isn't this just one more of the same?"

Twenty miles later, almost without realizing what she was doing, she made a U-turn and headed back to the camp. "I was following instinct, not reason. I drove into that wet and soggy camp and parked my car like a homing pigeon."

Migrant Mother (1), Nipomo, California, 1936

Migrant Mother (2), Nipomo, California, 1936

A string of dirty tents sprawled across a desolate field, pitched on the bare, wet ground with no wooden floors to keep out the dampness. Piles of rubbish were heaped behind the tents. Old ramshackle cars were parked in the mud. Just a stone's throw away was the prosperous, cozy town of Nipomo. The small town ignored the migrants' camp that had sprung up next to them, uninvited and unwanted.

A woman and her four children sat listlessly in a lean-to shelter on the edge of the camp. Dorothea went straight to them with her camera. The woman didn't ask any questions, but she told Dorothea that freezing rain and sleet had ruined the pea crop. There was no work, and they had just sold the tires from the car to buy food. For the past several weeks they had been living on frozen vegetables from the fields. In the camp at Shafter, California, the older children had learned to

3

Migrant Mother (4), Nipomo, California, 1936

throw rocks at the small sparrows, killing them and knocking them out of the low, branching trees. When the sparrows were cooked up in a stew, the younger children didn't realize what they were eating. But at the Nipomo camp, with only tall eucalyptus trees nearby, even these morsels of bird meat were unobtainable.

Dorothea took only a few pictures, moving closer and closer to the desperate and hungry family. Then she packed up her camera without approaching any of the other pea pickers. It wasn't necessary. She knew she had just recorded the essence of her month-long assignment. She climbed back into her car and headed for home.

Waking early the next morning, Dorothea pushed aside her deep weariness and hurried into the darkroom. Haunted by what she had seen at the pea pickers' camp, she knew she needed to act immediately. Being with her family would have to wait. Making prints of the migrant mother and her children was more important.

With the photographs barely dry, she rushed to the city editor of the *San Francisco News* and told him that rain had ruined the pea crop, stranding several thousand pea pickers. Tires, clothes, and even bedding had been sold just to buy a little food. The paper ran the story on March 10, using her photos. The article was picked up and carried in newspapers across the country.

The response to the newspaper article was instantaneous and powerful. Seeing the desperate, helpless mother unable to feed her children shocked Americans nationwide. They were appalled that the very people who provided food for American families were themselves starving. The federal government acted immediately, shipping twenty thousand pounds of food to the California fields.

Dorothea felt a flood of relief and satisfaction that she had helped the starving pea pickers. But she had no way of knowing then that *Migrant Mother* would become her most famous image, reproduced thousands of times all over the world. To many, it came to symbolize the despair and uncertainty of the Great Depression.

Dorothea continued as a photographer until her death in 1965, crisscrossing America, and later the world, with her camera. Some of her most revealing images are her photographs of children. With patience and compassion, she captured the quiet sorrows and joys of children everywhere. Their vulnerability must have touched the tender, unprotected places Dorothea carried inside from her own childhood. She knew, firsthand, the courage it took to meet bitter times.

Dorothea and Martin, ca. 1905 (Photographer unknown)

CHAPTER ONE

LIMPY

*"I've never gotten over it, and I am aware of
the force and the power of it."*

Dorothea was fourteen when she stood in the back parlor with her mother's friend, staring out the window. It was washday, and laundry hung from the high line strung across the backyard. The wash flapped and billowed in the breeze, making vivid patterns against the late afternoon sky. A rusty squeaking from the line filled the air.

"To me, that's beautiful," Dorothea said, breaking her reverie.

The friend replied, "To you, everything is beautiful."

That surprised Dorothea. "I thought everyone saw everything I saw and didn't talk about it." It also helped her. "It made me aware that maybe I had eyesight."

Dorothea lived in Hoboken, New Jersey, a quiet port town just across the Hudson River from New York City. Her grandparents had come to America in the huge immigrant wave from Europe in the mid 1800s. Like many German immigrants, the whole family came together, leaving the streets of Stuttgart and crowding into the steerage compartment of an ocean liner for the long trip across the cold, stormy Atlantic.

Whether it was the long, rough passage in steerage that wore them out, or fear of their new, English-speaking country, Dorothea's grandparents never budged once they got to Hoboken.

Dorothea's father, Henry Nutzhorn, was a lawyer, and her mother, Joan, sang soprano in local concerts. They married on May 27, 1894, and lived in a handsome brownstone house on Bloomfield Street. Just a year later, on May 25, 1895, their daughter was born. They named her Dorothea Margaretta Nutzhorn after Henry's grandmother, Dorothea Fischer. In 1901, when Dorothea was six, her parents had a boy, Martin.

A year after Martin was born, Dorothea came down with polio. There was no prevention for this crippling illness at that time, and no cure. For many days a fever raged through her body. Her head, back, and legs ached terribly. When the fever finally broke, she was weak and exhausted, and her right leg was permanently damaged.

For the rest of her life she walked with a rolling gait, dropping her left shoulder slightly as she pulled her right foot forward. "I think it perhaps was the most important thing that happened to me. It formed me, guided me, instructed me, helped me, and humiliated me. All those things at once. I've never gotten over it, and I am aware of the force and the power of it."

Dorothea wasn't able to run and jump as she had before. Quick to pick up on her difference, the other children in the neighborhood began calling her "Limpy." Dorothea's mother made things even worse. Appearances were important to her. When she was out walking with Dorothea in Hoboken and someone they knew approached, Joan would lean over to whisper in Dorothea's ear, "Now walk as well as you can!"

The words stung Dorothea. She was already concentrating, putting every ounce of effort into moving as normally as possible. But it wasn't good enough. She thought her mother was ashamed of her, and she felt bitter inside. For the rest of her life, Dorothea would say to herself, "Not good enough, Dorothea, not good enough."

Dorothea and Martin called their mother "the Wuz," because she could be so indecisive and vague, so "wuzzy." When Joan took Dorothea to see the doctors about her polio, Joan deferred to them in ways that bothered Dorothea. She hated the way her mother cared about what others thought, and how she had an automatic respect for any kind of authority.

Dorothea knew from early on that she and her mother were very different. "I have more iron," Dorothea explained. "Maybe I can be more cruel. Maybe it is in my independence, which is more than she had."

My Mother, the "Wuz," 1920s

In the family's living room there was a huge volume of Shakespeare's plays. She would sit for hours with the heavy book open on her lap, carefully sounding out the words written in tiny print.

Her parents were sure Dorothea couldn't really understand Shakespearean English. When they found out she could, her father was astonished. He hired a splendid carriage pulled by two horses and took her to see Shakespeare's play *A Midsummer Night's Dream.*

But by the time they arrived, all the seats were taken. Her father stood in the back, holding her high on his shoulders for the whole performance. "It was a magic thing to do for me. Magic!" she said later. "I've always been grateful to him for that. And that coach!"

Dorothea never felt things halfway. On her tenth birthday, her uncle gave her a small bunch of lilacs. "I sat on the Twenty-third Street cross-town car with those lilacs in my lap, jammed in with people, feeling so wonderful. I can see myself. I had a straw hat on. I can hear the sounds of the horse-drawn cross-town. And the flowers—all my life I don't think I did get over it. I am a passionate lover of flowers. And that's the moment that did it."

When Dorothea was twelve, her father walked out on the family without warning. He sent no word of his whereabouts, or any money. Joan and the children had to move in with her mother, Dorothea's grandmother, Sophie Lange.

Sophie was a tiny woman who dressed in black. She had a fierce temper. She was a "temperamental, talented woman," said Dorothea. "She was a dressmaker, a very good one, but she was difficult." Sophie spoke a little English but mostly spoke in her German dialect. She was blunt and uncompromising. When she wanted to get rid of company at the end of the evening she would say, "Let's go to bed so the people can go home."

Grandmother Sophie (Photographer and date unknown)

Joan's timid nature made her retreat into herself. She could not stand up to her own mother. In contrast, there were ways Dorothea felt especially well understood by her grandmother, as difficult as she was. "My mother was her only daughter and they were devoted to each other," Dorothea said. "But my grandmother knew that I was smarter than my mother, more sensitive."

One day when Dorothea was

watching her grandmother sew, she overheard her say to Joan, "That girl has line in her head." Sophie meant that Dorothea had a sense of "what was fine and what was mongrel, what was pure and what was corrupted in things, and in workmanship."

With her husband gone, Joan had to become the breadwinner—and quickly—for the family. She got a job at the New York Public Library, working on the Lower East Side, earning fifty-five dollars a month, a decent wage in 1907. In the morning Dorothea and her mother would take the ferry into New York City. Dorothea went to school while her mother worked.

There was a huge difference between the quiet town of Hoboken and the crowded, chaotic bedlam of the Lower East side. Thousands of immigrants were

My Childhood Home, 1960s

"I was struck down by polio in this house. And in this house I lived until a certain very bad thing happened to my family. I was then twelve years old."

The Lower East Side of Manhattan, early 1900s. (Photographer unknown)

flooding into the Lower East Side every day, making it one of the most congested square miles in the world. Eastern European Jews, Italians, Irish, Slavs, and Russians made up the crowds that pushed and shoved their way through the neighborhood. Vendors jammed the streets with their pushcarts, hawking their wares in all kinds of languages. Jewish women wearing black wigs called *schachtels* bargained noisily with the vendors, and boys in ragged clothes sold daily newspapers for a penny each. The smells of foreign cooking filled the air—cabbage, corned beef, pickles, and potatoes.

More than half of the children crammed into the crowded buildings of New York City did not go to school. They had to work so their families could survive.

Often they earned as little as thirty cents a day, working ten or twelve hours in cramped, poorly lit sweatshops.

Dorothea went to Public School 62, which she called a "great, big educational factory." She was a poor student, finding school boring and stifling. Dorothea was one of a few Gentiles in a school of three thousand Jewish children. "I was an outsider," she recalled. "I was unhappy there, but I had to stay."

She did make one friend, Florence Alstrom, who sat in front of her at school. "Fronsie" had long, dark curls and swished her petticoat as she walked through the halls. Dorothea admired her spirit.

But most of the time Dorothea was by herself. After school she would walk to the library and wait for her mother so they could go home together. "They were rather long walks in all seasons of the year, and I was always alone. I saw a very great deal." Though walking always required extra effort for Dorothea, she didn't let it stop her.

Once she got to the library, she was supposed to do her homework, but usually she didn't. "I remember spending as much time as I could neglecting what I should be doing—I didn't study well—looking at pictures. I looked and looked."

Two days a week her mother worked late, and Dorothea left the library alone at five o'clock. She had to walk through the Bowery, a crowded, rundown part of New York City known as "thieves' highway." Drunk men lay sprawled across the sidewalks, and nervous thieves tried to sell their stolen goods. Sour smells hung in the air. Garbage and dirt, caught by the wind, swirled up from the filthy gutters. "I remember how afraid I was each time, never without fear," said Dorothea.

Unable to move quickly, she had to find another way to feel safe. She learned how to make a bland facial expression that would draw no attention. It was a technique she would use all her life while photographing on the streets. "I can turn it off and on," she said once. "If I don't want anybody to see me, I can make the kind of face so nobody will look at me." She called it her "cloak of invisibility."

By the time Dorothea was in high school, her grandmother had become messy and disorderly, drinking too much and quarreling with anyone who crossed her. Sometimes when she was frustrated she would slap Dorothea and her brother Martin. Dorothea stayed out of the house as much as possible. "I fled," she said later. "I couldn't take these things."

The Bowery, early 1900s. (Photographer unknown)

"On the Bowery I knew how to step over drunken men. I knew how to keep an expression of face that would draw no attention, so no one would look at me. I have used that my whole life in photographing."

Restlessly, she'd set out for Wadleigh High School for Girls, but partway there she'd impulsively turn and walk in another direction, her books cradled in one arm. She loved walking alone all day through the city, taking in the noise and squalor and teeming beauty of the streets. She would slip into museums and concerts, or walk the length of Central Park. Sometimes she'd convince her friend Fronsie to join her, but usually she was by herself.

Dorothea's mother never knew that she was cutting school. "I was essentially neglected, thank God!" Dorothea said. "Not deprived of love, but they just didn't know where I was or how I was living. I realize how enriched I am through having been on the loose in my formative years. I have known all my life so many

14

people who have always done what they should do, been proper, made the grades—and lost."

When she finished high school in 1914, Dorothea's grades were barely good enough for her to graduate. "What are you going to do?" her mother asked anxiously.

"I want to be a photographer," Dorothea declared.

She had never taken a picture or owned a camera, but her years of looking at everything had created a passionate desire to make her own photographs.

Joan had a different plan. She wanted her daughter to become a teacher, so that she would have something "to fall back on." That sounded dangerous to Dorothea. If she settled for "something to fall back on," she might not go all out for her dreams.

But Joan, usually so pliant, put her foot down. She insisted that Dorothea enroll in a school for teachers.

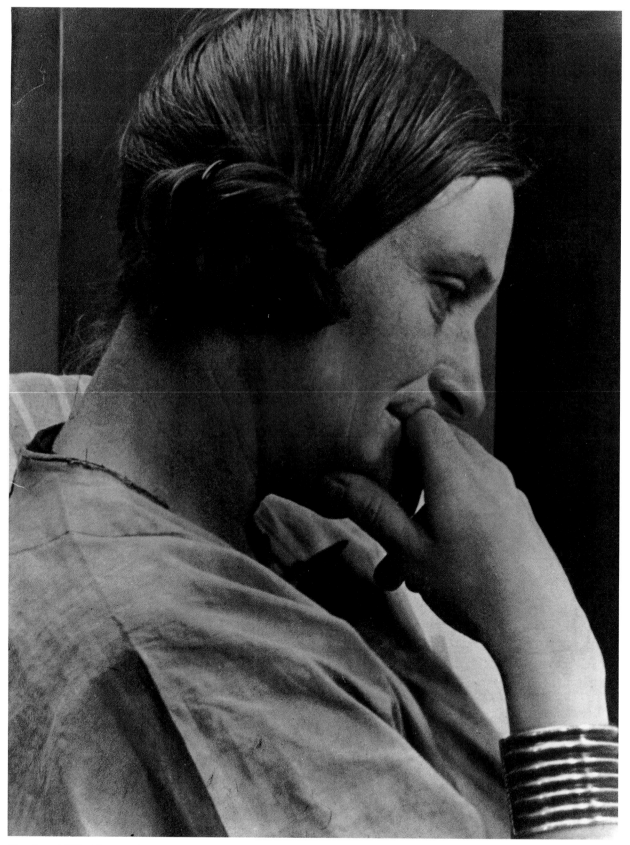

Dorothea, 1920s (Photographer unknown)

CHAPTER TWO

PORTRAIT PHOTOGRAPHER

"I really and seriously tried, with every person I photographed,
to reveal them as closely as I could."

Reluctantly, Dorothea enrolled in the New York Training School for Teachers. She hated the dreary classrooms and the long corridors, the change of classes with the crowded halls, and the noise.

Although Joan seriously misjudged Dorothea's interests, she was right about the limited job opportunities for women. At the time, only one in four women worked outside the home. The most common jobs they held were, in this order, servant, teacher, farm laborer, typist, clerk, and laundry worker.

Despite her time commitment to the school, Dorothea was determined to learn photography. She began at the top, going to Arnold Genthe's studio on Fifth Avenue and asking him for a job. Genthe was famous for his pictures of the 1906 San Francisco earthquake. By the time Dorothea approached him, he had established a large and wealthy portrait clientele in New York City.

Genthe hired Dorothea on the spot. Something in her intense, earnest appeal for work must have convinced him to give her a job even though she had no training or experience in photography.

Every day after school, she worked in Genthe's studio, often staying late into the evening. Oriental rugs covered the floor, and beautiful paintings hung on the walls. Wealthy people and celebrities had their portraits taken by Genthe, people like Presidents Roosevelt, Taft, and Wilson, and movie stars like Mary Pickford, Greta Garbo, and John Barrymore. The studio offered a look into a privileged

Portrait Photograph of Arnold Genthe Taken Outdoors
(Photographer and date unknown)

world Dorothea hadn't seen before. It seemed to her "the most miraculous kind of living, very luxurious, everything of the highest expression." It was an enormous change from the impoverished streets of the Lower East Side, and the dull, middle-class streets of Hoboken.

Genthe taught Dorothea how to set up lights and operate the large, cumbersome cameras. She learned to "spot" the prints, which meant using a delicate brush and India ink to cover the tiny white specks on the prints left by dust. Genthe paid her fifteen dollars a week, not a bad wage for the time. While she was working, Dorothea was interacting with some of the richest and most influential people in New York, and learning how to cater to the whims of these wealthy customers.

Eager to learn all she could, Dorothea went on to work for several other studios over the next few years. "I invented my own photographic schooling as I went along," she said, "stumbling into most of it."

She did take one photography class at Columbia University. It was taught by Clarence White, a small, gentle, inarticulate photographer. He had a fine, absolute sense of what was beautiful and struggled to teach his students how to capture it

18

on film. Dorothea, never willing to follow instructions, didn't do a single assignment he gave the class. He didn't seem to mind. She went faithfully to each class meeting, however, absorbing his unconscious, instinctive way of living the life of a photographer.

During this time, Dorothea had to student teach fifth grade as part of her teacher's training. Left alone with the students on her first day, she wasn't able to control the classroom, and she watched helplessly as the students climbed out the window and ran down the fire escape to get down to the playground. Soon the entire classroom was empty. Dorothea, humiliated and angry, was in tears when the teaching supervisor entered the room.

She went home and confronted her mother. Teaching was unbearable, and she clearly wasn't suited for it. By now, Joan was resigned to Dorothea's being "independent and impractical." Dorothea dropped out of school and bought a view camera with bellows that pleated out, and two lenses. "I photographed people whom we knew, and then children," she said. "It was a very restricted range of people because I was just trying it out." She wasn't trying to be an artist, she wanted to be a portrait photographer. "It was a good trade, one I could do. It was a choice. I picked it."

One day a traveling photographer came to the door, offering to make inexpensive family snapshots. As they talked, Dorothea found out that he didn't have his own darkroom. She offered him the old, unused chicken coop in her backyard. Together they turned it into a darkroom. They swept out the old straw, feathers, and droppings and put up heavy black paper to keep out all the light. He taught her how to develop her photographs in the darkroom, and soon she was working on her own.

With the darkroom lit only by the soft yellow glow of a "safe light," Dorothea took the negatives from their holders and developed them in baths of sharp-smelling chemicals. The image would appear in reverse—the lighted areas were dark, and the dark areas were light.

When the negative was dry she put a sheet of photographic paper tightly against it and briefly exposed it to bright light. Then she dropped the paper into the bath of developer, rocking it gently. Every so often she would pull out the paper by a corner, flip it over, and push it gently back into the chemical bath with her fingertips. Slowly, ghostly gray smudges would appear on the paper, sharpening into the image. She'd pull the print out, dripping wet, and examine it by the safe light, her face close to the wet photograph in the soft, diffuse light.

Dorothea didn't have a natural aptitude for working in a darkroom. She referred to the "terrors of the darkroom," because she was always afraid of making mistakes, always worried that her work would be wasted. But she kept at it. Photography "is a gambler's game," she explained. "I have a streak of that gambler."

Finally she had all the skills she needed to set up her own studio. But Dorothea knew she needed to get away from Hoboken, New Jersey, to prove herself. "I wanted to go away as far as I could go," said Dorothea. "Not that I was bitterly unhappy at home, or doing what I was doing. But it was a matter of really testing yourself out. Could you or couldn't you?"

In January 1918, at the age of twenty-two, Dorothea persuaded her friend Fronsie to go around the world with her. They pooled their money—$140—and headed west with two suitcases. Their first day in San Francisco, a thief slipped his hand into Fronsie's pocket and stole the wallet holding all their money.

The next morning they checked into the Episcopal Home for Working Girls and went looking for jobs. Dorothea opened a phone book and looked up the places that did photofinishing, knowing she could get a job right away. By that evening, both she and Fronsie were employed. Dorothea found work at the photofinishing counter in a department store, and Fronsie took a job at Western Union, sending telegrams.

San Francisco immediately suited Dorothea's temperament. It was a lively, free-spirited city. Bankers, merchants, and wealthy miners ran profitable businesses downtown. Various ethnic groups set up enclaves: Little Mexico, Little Italy, Chinatown. Ranchers, cowboys, and lumberjacks poured into town looking for a good time, and the docks swarmed with sailors from all over the world. Rudyard Kipling called it "a mad city, inhabited by perfectly insane people whose women are of a remarkable beauty."

It was also a city that loved and supported its artists. Painters, writers, poets, musicians, and playwrights thrived in San Francisco. They called themselves Bohemians.

The very first day on her new job Dorothea met Roi Partridge, an etcher, and his wife, photographer Imogen Cunningham. They became fast friends. In no time, they introduced her to other artists, and she was quickly included in the Bohemian art crowd. Dorothea called the Bohemians "the free and easy livers. They were people who lived according to their own standards and did what they wanted to do in the way they wanted to do it."

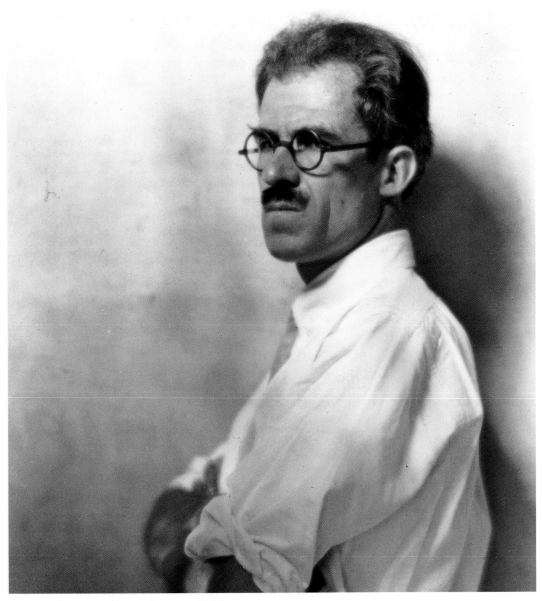

Portrait of Roi Partridge, San Francisco, 1925
"No subject can hold anything that is false for them for long. So you have to wait until certain decisions are made by the subject. What is he going to give to the camera? And the photographer, what is he going to take?"

Caught up in her new life, Dorothea made some swift changes. Still wounded to the quick by her father's abandonment, she dropped her last name, Nutzhorn, and took on her mother's maiden name, Lange. Her father's desertion was one of her most painful secrets. Why should she carry his name? She never spoke of him or told her new friends that she had been named Nutzhorn.

Another secret she carried deeply was how much she hated her disability. Getting on an elevator one day, Dorothea was joined by a woman with a limp that was much worse than hers. Filled with a surge of self-loathing for her own lameness, Dorothea decided at that moment to get rid of her limp. She begged her new friends Imogen and Roi to take ballroom dancing with her, thinking it would improve the way she moved. She practiced diligently, struggling to control her legs. Though she learned to move more gracefully, she was unable to overcome her limp.

To hide her limp, she began wearing long, swirling skirts. She wore heavy, primitive silver jewelry and a black beret cocked casually over one ear.

Dorothea longed to open her own portrait studio. But setting up a studio was very expensive. Jack Boumphrey, a "wildly rich" Irishman visiting friends of Dorothea's, liked both Dorothea and Fronsie very much. He offered Dorothea a three-thousand-dollar loan to start her business. Dorothea jumped at the chance, and after having been in San Francisco for only six months, she rented part of a beautiful building on Sutter Street and opened her studio.

The main floor had a large, open room with a fireplace at one end. In front of the fireplace she set up an enormous black velvet couch with plump, down-filled cushions. Downstairs she built a darkroom. She hired a helper and began taking portraits. She photographed one of the wealthiest women in San Francisco, who was delighted with the results. Word spread quickly, and Dorothea became the favorite photographer of the well-to-do.

The entire first session with a new client might go by without Dorothea taking a single picture. She would gently ask questions, listening earnestly to the responses, trying to get a feel for the person. By the time she did photograph, people were comfortable being themselves in front of her camera. They felt Dorothea understood them and that her photographs would reveal their true essences.

Determined to make her studio a success, Dorothea worked long hours, up to

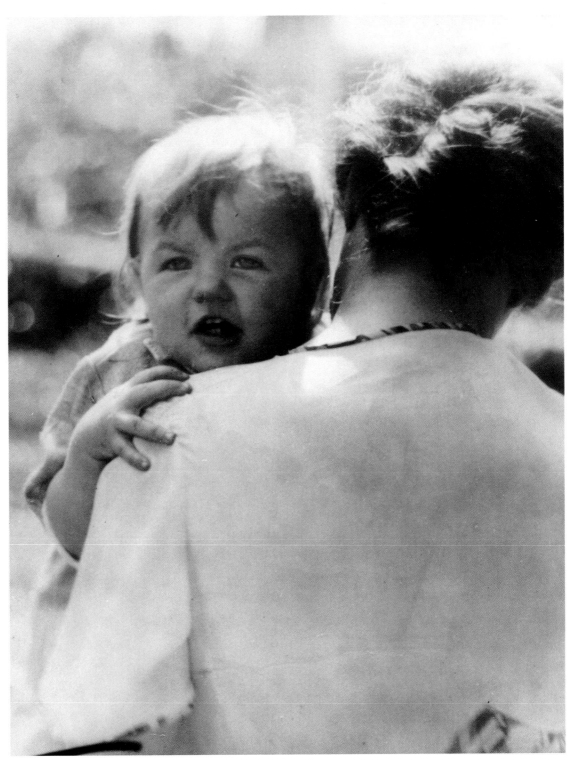

Gertrude Clausen Holding Nancy, studio portrait, 1932

Mrs. Kahn and Child, San Francisco, studio portrait, 1928

the limits of her endurance. Many evenings, weekends, and holidays she spent in the darkroom, developing the photographs she had taken.

At five every day Dorothea's helper made tea in a big brass Russian samovar, an ornate teapot kept steaming hot by piling coals underneath. Artists of all kinds gathered, drinking tea, talking, and dancing to the latest jazz music. Often they began arriving while Dorothea was still working downstairs in her darkroom. She learned to recognize their footsteps overhead.

"One night there came some very peculiar sharp, clicking footsteps, and I wondered who that was," she said. "A couple of nights later I heard the same steps."

She was listening to Maynard Dixon walk overhead. He was one of the most

24

colorful characters of Bohemian San Francisco. Handsome and fiercely independent, he was a painter, filling huge canvases with scenes of the rugged, untamed West.

"He wore cowboy boots with very high heels, Texas boots," Dorothea said. "For a while I was very much afraid of those footsteps and when I heard them I wouldn't go upstairs. I avoided him." But despite her trepidation, something in the strong, insistent footsteps drew her to him.

Dorothea in the Kitchen, 1936 (Photograph by Ron Partridge)

CHAPTER THREE

CONFLICTING DEMANDS

"The woman's position is immeasurably more complicated."

The tangy smell of paint and turpentine clung to Maynard Dixon as he strode into Dorothea's studio. Sitting on the black velvet couch, he would roll a cigarette of pipe tobacco, sagebrush, and manzanita bark, called kinnikinnick. The other artists gathered around him.

In a cloud of blue smoke he recounted vivid stories from his childhood. Born in California in 1875, Maynard remembered a time when posses still tracked down stagecoach robbers, and Apaches raided white settlements in Arizona. At seven Maynard began drawing. When he was ten, his father took him to Yosemite in a wagon, bumping roughly over an old wagon trail. By sixteen he had dropped out of school to study art on his own. He often took long, solitary sketching trips into the mountains and deserts, where he stayed with cowboys and Native Americans.

Despite Dorothea's initial fear, she was fascinated by Maynard. She admired his sharp wit, his rich, detailed stories, and his ability to draw anything—quickly and effortlessly—with his long, slim left hand. "He was the kind legends cluster about, without his making any particular effort," she said later. "I have never watched any person's life as closely as I watched his, what it held, how he lived it."

Six months after meeting Maynard, Dorothea told her friend Imogen that she was going to marry him. "I told her Maynard was too old," said Imogen. "But she didn't listen." Dorothea didn't care that she was only twenty-four and Maynard was forty-five.

With Fronsie as the maid of honor and Roi Partridge as the best man, Dorothea and Maynard were married on March 21, 1920. They made a striking couple: Maynard tall and arrow-thin, casually carrying a silver-tipped cane; Dorothea, short and compact, with her beautiful silver necklace and long, fluid skirt.

Maynard Dixon at His Easel, ca. 1920
"Curiously enough, when he was with the cowboys he was the sophisticated artist, while when he was with the artists he was the cowboy."

They rented a tiny, one-bedroom house perched on a steep hillside between their two studios. Orange nasturtiums edged the tall wooden steps rising sharply up to their new home. To fight the constant gray fog that drifted in from the bay, Maynard and Dorothea painted their floor a deep, indigo blue and dyed the curtains bright yellow.

With her marriage came new responsibilities that cut deeply into her time for photography. From his first marriage Maynard had a ten-year-old daughter, Consie, who came to live with them. Maynard left Consie's care entirely up to Dorothea.

Dorothea had sympathy for Consie's difficult position, so she threw herself into the task of being a good stepmother. Feeling that Consie had been neglected, Dorothea took her to art galleries, concerts, and lectures. At home she struggled to teach Consie good housekeeping skills: washing, cooking, ironing, and cleaning.

Consie with Maynard's Horse, ca. 1920

Dorothea no longer lit the samovar and welcomed her friends for tea and dancing. She had to rush home at five to make dinner. She demanded Consie's help. But when Consie didn't do exactly as she was told—peeling carrots a certain way, for example—Dorothea would explode in a rage. She would lash out at Consie, sometimes even slapping her.

Filled with remorse afterward, Dorothea would break down and cry, begging Consie not to tell Maynard. Dorothea was deeply ashamed of herself; she was acting just like her grandmother. But even when she tried to be more patient, she wasn't able to control her temper. Soon Consie was sent to live with nearby family friends, the Wilsons. "Daddy" and Mary Ann Wilson had a daughter of their own and didn't mind having Consie stay with them. Frightened by Dorothea's temper, Consie must have been relieved to go.

Maynard and John at Alta, 1929

On May 15, 1925, Maynard and Dorothea had a son, Daniel. At first, Dorothea was uneasy handling her new baby. "Don't worry," said Maynard. "Treat him just the same as a puppy."

Three years later, on June 12, 1928, they had a second son, John. Life became quite a bit more complicated for Dorothea. "I had a family to hold together, and little boys to rear without disturbing Maynard too much, though he was very good to us."

In addition to caring for her family and running her studio, Dorothea liked to lead a gracious social life, often with people she considered "top-drawer." Maynard found "the fancy life" pretentious and couldn't resist poking fun at Dorothea. Once, at a small dinner party, Maynard taught Imogen and Roi Partridge's young son Rondal a dirty rhyme in the kitchen, then sent him out to repeat it to the guests. Dorothea was furious.

Often Maynard went out of town on painting expeditions. Though not a solitary man, he liked a certain amount of solitude. He'd pack his paints and take off for the desert, saying he would be gone for four to six weeks, but he rarely came back in less than six months. Dorothea missed him when he was gone and was glad when he returned. Life was much more exciting when he was around.

When the boys got a little older, Maynard got hold of two old, beat-up saddles and nailed them to the low wooden fence. They were a magnet for the kids in the neighborhood. Sitting up on those saddles, the kids pretended to be riding out with a posse, rustling cattle, or running free as outlaws. In the middle of the garden, Maynard put up a real tepee for the boys to play in.

The newspapers, always interested in the Bohemians, sent a reporter to ask Dorothea how she managed being married to an artist. "Simple," responded Dorothea. "Simple that is, when an artist's wife accepts the fact that he needs a certain amount of freedom—freedom from the petty, personal things of life."

Unfortunately, Dorothea didn't have an equal measure of freedom. She began her days by getting the household chores done, arranging for the care of the boys, organizing their meals, then hurrying to her studio. After work she rushed home, made dinner, and devoted the evening to her boys. Sometimes she photographed at home, but not often. One year she picked up her camera to capture the fistful of daisies John gathered for Mother's Day and held out to her.

Mother's Day Daisies, 1934

At the time when Dorothea was a young mother, there was a clear expectation that women would stay home and care for their families. If they worked outside the home (either by choice or necessity), they had the double burden of managing a career and carrying all the responsibilities for the household at the same time. Men were not expected to help. It was not surprising that tensions broke out between Maynard and Dorothea. They quarreled frequently.

To give her full attention to her work, Dorothea began having the boys stay with different families for days or even weeks at a time. Sometimes they stayed with the Wilsons, who had Consie, or with Dorothea's brother, Martin, who had left New Jersey and lived in nearby San Jose.

The family was together in San Francisco when the stock market crashed on October 24, 1929. The nation plunged into desperate financial times. Factories closed. New construction came to a standstill, and banks quit lending money. People were laid off work. The Great Depression had begun. In just a few years, one out of every four workers would no longer have a job.

It became much more difficult for Dorothea and Maynard to make a living. Wealthy people ordered fewer portraits, and it was hard to sell paintings. Childhood asthma and smoking kinnikinnick were taking a toll on Maynard. He developed emphysema, and any exertion made him short of breath. Tense and worried about money, he and Dorothea clashed more frequently.

In the summer of 1931 they bought a secondhand model A Ford from the San Francisco Police Department and drove to Taos, New Mexico. Dan was six and John three. "We weren't there because of the Depression but because Maynard wanted to paint and there was enough money to see us through. The outside world was full of uncertainty and unrest and trouble and we got in that car and we went and we stayed there."

In Taos they rented an adobe house set alone on the top of a hill. The earth was red-brown under an endless, deep blue sky. The thick-walled house sheltered them from the wind that swept over, blowing through the cottonwood and poplar trees.

Every day Dorothea drove Maynard to his studio in town. He painted the vast, desert expanses and the rugged mesas with their long, blue shadows. Silent Native Americans and horses moved slowly across the foreground of his canvases.

Maynard and Dan Painting, early 1930s
"All the years that I lived with Maynard I continued to reserve a small portion of my life, and that was my photographic area. Still, my deepest allegiances were to Maynard's work, and my children."

As soon as Dorothea returned from Maynard's studio, she plunged into household chores. She pumped water from the well to clean, wash clothes, and scrub. Filling the fireplace with mesquite wood, she made hearty lamb and bean stews. Then at the end of the day she went back into town to pick up Maynard.

For the boys, this was the most time they had ever spent with their mother. They were given a gentle Indian pony and learned to ride bareback. At Christmastime they cut down a juniper tree in the woods and decorated it with painted pinecones and feathers and bits of wood.

Southwest, ca. 1930

"We went into a country which was endless and timeless. The earth and the heavens, even the change of seasons, I'd never really experienced until that time. Then I became aware."

Occasionally Dorothea took photographs of her children or of the people in town, but immersing herself in her work was not possible. Between Maynard and the boys, there were endless demands on her time.

Every morning she watched another photographer, Paul Strand, drive by her house on the way to his studio, and then drive home again at the end of the day. She was painfully aware of the difference between male and female artists. "There is a sharp difference, a gulf. The woman's position is immeasurably more complicated. What Paul Strand was able to do, I wasn't."

Hopi Man, 1920s

As winter came, the temperature fell below zero. Maynard's lungs worsened in the freezing cold. Even when he bundled up in three layers of clothes and two pairs of gloves, he was too cold to paint. It was time to go home.

They packed up the car and drove out through the deep, glittering snow. They were the first to break the trail that winter. If they had strayed from the road they would have fallen off the sheer mountainside and tumbled hundreds of feet down to the Rio Grande.

Back in San Francisco they made a wrenching decision. They would live separately, Maynard in his studio, Dorothea in hers. Although Dan was seven and John only four, they were sent to boarding school. Living this way, Dorothea explained, they would save the expenses of renting a house and running a household. It may also have been a trial separation, but they told their friends only that they were trying to save money.

On weekends Dorothea and Maynard visited the boys at school. Long before their parents arrived, John and Dan ran outside and stood by the side of the road. They waited, anxious and excited, for the first glimpse of the car.

Dorothea and Maynard arrived in the Model A Ford, bringing a knapsack bulging with food: a thick steak, sliced cucumbers, cheese, and bread. They'd drive into the empty, grass-covered hills, eat grilled steak off tin plates, and practice target shooting with Maynard's Colt .44 pistol.

"Always take your time," Maynard told the boys when they aimed the heavy

Maynard and Boys, End of the Visit, ca. 1934

pistol. "That's what Wyatt Earp always said, and it's good advice."

Soon the visit was over, and the boys were taken back. Once again they stood by the road, this time with a terrible, lonely feeling, weeping as they watched the red taillights on the Ford disappear in the distance.

Being separated from her children was painful for Dorothea. "This was very, very hard for me to do," Dorothea said years later. "Even now when I speak of it I feel the pain. I carry these things inside and it hurts me in the same spot that it did then."

Dorothea Lange, 1934 (Photograph by Paul S. Taylor)

CHAPTER FOUR

TO THE STREETS

"Everyone was so shocked and panicky. No one knew what was ahead."

Back in her studio without the boys to care for, Dorothea was free to spend long hours making portraits for the people who could still afford them. But her attention turned to the despair and unrest seething in the streets below.

When she looked down from her second-story studio window, she saw hungry, homeless men wandering forlornly along the sidewalks. Sometimes they stopped at the corner outside her studio and looked around uncertainly, not sure where to go next. Other times they stood in groups, talking angrily, afraid of what was happening to them, to the whole country.

More than fifteen million people were out of work. Children went to bed at night, bellies aching with hunger. Drifters—more than two million of them—rode the trains or hitchhiked aimlessly from place to place, looking for odd jobs or a free meal at one of the soup kitchens. More than 250 thousand of these drifters were children. Some were with their parents, but many were teenage boys cut loose from their families to fend for themselves.

One autumn day as Dorothea looked out her window, she was seized with the urge to photograph what she was watching. She wasn't sure exactly what to photograph, or why. She only knew she felt driven to do something. "I went out just absolutely in the blind staggers," she said.

Dorothea took her camera and walked over to Market Street where a woman called the White Angel ran a soup kitchen. Hungry people lined up early to get a free meal from her kitchen. Dorothea set up her camera and photographed men eating stew and bread from battered plates, washed down with weak cups of coffee. Some men wore fancy homburg hats and their best suits, now dirty and rumpled from being slept in beside the road or under a bridge.

As Dorothea looked through the lens of her camera, she had a shock of recognition. These were people who had once led successful lives—bankers, small businessmen, farmers. Now they had no jobs, no homes, no hope.

Perhaps Dorothea remembered her childhood walks along the Bowery. Now, as then, she was not one of the down-and-outers, but moved among them quietly, invisibly, a little bit afraid. "I was just gathering my forces and that took a little bit because I wasn't accustomed to jostling about in groups of tormented, depressed, and angry men, with a camera."

Dorothea made a print of the White Angel bread line and put it up on the wall of her studio. Her wealthy clients asked, "What are you going to do with it?" She didn't have the slightest idea.

Hesitantly at first, Dorothea took her camera to the roughest parts of town, which were filled with the unemployed and homeless. "Don't go there," friends urged her. But she felt compelled to leave the safe, orderly life of her studio. The Depression "was beginning to cut very deep. This is a long process. It doesn't happen overnight. Life, for people, begins to crumble on the edges."

Dorothea wanted to document the disastrous human consequences of the Depression. She photographed the "hobo jungles," where men and boys threw together makeshift camps, the soup lines and the unemployed, hopeless people who had drifted all the way west to San Francisco.

The more she worked outside her studio, the more clear she was about what she was looking for. She photographed a man sitting with his head in his hands, his upside-down wheelbarrow next to him. Earlier, she would have just taken a picture of the man. No more. Now she wanted to take a more complete picture of him. He was "a man with his head down, with his back against the wall, with his livelihood, like his wheelbarrow, overturned."

While Dorothea was spending more time photographing out on the streets, she and Maynard decided to make a last effort to keep their marriage together. They rented a house on Gough Street and brought the boys home to live with

White Angel Bread Line, San Francisco, 1933

Man Beside Wheelbarrow, San Francisco, 1934

them. Dan and John were overjoyed that the family was back together.

Dorothea sometimes took Dan and John to the Crystal Palace Plunge, an indoor swimming pool with a glass roof. The air inside was warm and the daylight looked soft and filmy. In the pool, Dorothea wasn't limited by her polio, which otherwise kept her from running and jumping with her boys. She swam a strong, relaxed sidestroke, splashing and playing with Dan and John while they dog-paddled happily around her.

At Christmastime Maynard cleaned up his studio. He and Dorothea put boards across sawhorses, covered them with beautiful white tablecloths, and gathered with friends for Christmas dinner.

Despite all they did as a family, Dorothea and Maynard were not as close as she would have liked. "I knew that this man loved me and was very, very good to me," she said. "Still, the depths of his life he didn't share with me. I wasn't really involved in the vitals of the man, not in the vitals."

As winter turned to spring, Dorothea kept a careful eye on the presidential race. On March 4, 1933, Franklin D. Roosevelt was inaugurated as president. Like Dorothea, he had been stricken with polio. But the damage to his legs was much worse than the damage to Dorothea's. He was paralyzed from the waist down. It had taken him years to learn to walk even a short distance, using heavy metal braces and a cane. The courage he had shown in overcoming polio made people feel he could understand their suffering and poverty.

Roosevelt promised "a new deal for the American people." In his first hundred days in office he put bill after bill through Congress, taking swift measures to provide jobs and relief. In late March, Congress approved Roosevelt's plan to establish the Civilian Conservation Corps (CCC). About 250,000 teenagers and young men

Homeless Boy and Cat at a CCC Camp, California, ca. 1934

One of the Wandering Homeless Boys, ca. 1934

were hired to do construction and conservation work. They worked ten hour days, slept in barracks or tents, and got three meals a day. They were paid thirty dollars a month, most of which had to be sent to their parents. In May, Congress passed a law giving $500 million in aid to the Federal Emergency Relief Administration (FERA).

Dorothea kept up a grueling schedule, photographing out on the streets and keeping her studio running. She wished she didn't have to continue making portraits, but her studio work paid many of the bills and helped finance Maynard's painting trips through the West.

She continued to send Dan and John to stay with other people when she needed to devote herself to her photography. The boys hated moving from place to place. They wanted to be home with their parents. They never knew when they would be boarded out again, or where they would go. Perhaps if they could have stayed with one family every time, it would have been easier. But that wasn't possible, and Dorothea was adamant about having enough time for her work. "Artists are controlled by the life that beats in them, like the ocean beats on the shore," she said. And the desire beating within her was the urge to be out on the streets, photographing.

In San Francisco, tensions continued to mount, despite the exciting changes put in place by Roosevelt. Millions were still unemployed. Many of the people who had jobs were paid very low wages and worked long, hard hours. If they didn't like it, all they could do was quit. There were plenty of other desperate, hungry people ready to take their places.

Early in May 1934, tempers boiled over in San Francisco. The longshoremen who loaded and unloaded the huge cargo ships coming into the busy port went out on strike. They had been working twenty-four to thirty-six hours at a stretch, doing hard, back-breaking work for terribly low wages. Weeks or months might pass before they were hired for another shift. They wanted higher wages, better

hours, and steadier work. Once they went on strike, the ship owners brought in other men to do their work, and violence broke out immediately. Dorothea picked up her camera and went out to photograph.

Imogen's son, Ron, wanted to go with Dorothea. He was sixteen years old and interested in being a photographer himself. He thought the strike was exciting. Dorothea refused to take him. "Too dangerous," she said. But that didn't stop her from going.

The strike spread, becoming a general strike that culminated in "Bloody Thursday," July 5, 1934. Bricks and tear gas filled the air, and policemen on horseback swung heavy clubs at the strikers. By the end of the day two strikers lay dead on the pavement.

The General Strike, (Policeman), San Francisco, 1934

Dorothea and Paul Taylor, 1939 (Photograph by Imogen Cunningham)

CHAPTER FIVE

STARVED, STALLED, AND STRANDED

"I had to get my camera to register the things that were more important than how poor they were—their pride, their strength, their spirit."

Dorothea and Maynard decided to take the boys up to Fallen Leaf Lake for the summer. They also took Roi and Imogen's twin sons, Ron and Pad. Maynard built an Indian-style sweat lodge and filled it with hot rocks from the campfire. Once the boys were hot and dripping with sweat in the lodge, they rushed out and dove into the icy lake water. This summer turned out to be one of the last times the family would be all together.

Though she longed to be down in San Francisco covering the waterfront strike, Dorothea tried to photograph where she was. Imogen was photographing plants—everything from delicate flower buds to prickly cacti. Her prints were luminous and beautiful. Another friend, Ansel Adams, was making spectacular landscape photographs of the wilderness. Both of them were showing their work in San Francisco art galleries.

Thinking of their work, Dorothea attempted to capture the beauty of nature that was all around her: the tall, weathered pines, the wide, delicate leaves of the skunk cabbage. But the photographs

Fallen Leaf Lake with the Partridge Boys, 1934

looked flat and empty to her. "Not good enough, Dorothea," she muttered to her-self. "Not good enough."

One afternoon, edgy and depressed about her work, she set out alone into the forest. A thunderstorm piled up. "When it broke, there I was, sitting on a big rock. And right in the middle of it, with the thunder bursting and the wind whistling, it came to me that what I had to do was to take pictures and concentrate upon people, only people, all kinds of people, people who paid me and people who didn't." Years later she told her son Dan that this was one of the great spiritual experiences of her life.

Down in the Bay Area, Dorothea's documentary photographs were being exhibited at a small gallery in Oakland. Paul Taylor, an economics professor at the nearby University of California, saw the show and was deeply impressed with her work. He was studying the self-help cooperatives that were springing up around the country. Under the slogan "Self-Help Beats Charity," people swapped services and goods as a way to get by without money. A mechanic might fix a bread truck in exchange for bakery goods, and a barber could give a family haircuts in trade for fruits and vegetables from their garden.

Paul called Dorothea to ask if she could go out in the field with him to photo-graph one of the cooperatives. Dorothea was eager to. In the fall, Paul took Dorothea, Imogen, and several other photographers to visit the Unemployed Exchange Association (UXA), a small self-help cooperative about 125 miles north of San Francisco. The UXA was made up of a group of families with many differ-ent skills who had banded together to run an old sawmill.

Paul and the photographers stayed for two days. Dorothea was fascinated by Paul's way of talking with the UXA workers, gently drawing information and feel-ings from them. Even when he wrote their responses down in a small black note-book they didn't seem to be self-conscious.

Dorothea learned about Paul's belief—that weaving each individual story together with all the other stories would clarify the larger issues America was struggling with. He was a "Jeffersonian" Democrat. Like Thomas Jefferson, Paul fervently believed that a sound democracy was based on having family-run farms and an elementary education for everyone.

While Dorothea watched Paul, he was also aware of her. He admired how she

Unemployed Exchange Association (UXA), Oroville, California, 1934

moved unobtrusively among the workers, speaking to no one, intently concentrating upon her photography. Her distinctive way of working appealed to him right away.

Driving to and from the UXA, Paul and the photographers found the roads swamped with old farm cars from out of state. Two or three generations were crammed together in each car. They looked tired, bewildered, and hungry. All the possessions they could stuff inside or lash on the outside of the car came with them: mattresses, an old iron stove, pots and pans, washbasins, lanterns, buckets, soap, and cardboard boxes full of clothing.

The federally funded State Emergency Relief Administration (SERA) didn't know what to do. They turned to Paul Taylor, who had a national reputation for his studies on rural poverty and migratory workers. Why were these people coming to California? Why were there so many?

Paul agreed to work part-time for SERA as a consultant. He would evaluate who had come to California, what their needs were, and how best to take care of them.

"But I'll need to hire a photographer," he said. "I'd like the people in the relief administration to see what the rural conditions are like. My words won't be enough to show the conditions visually and accurately." Paul wanted Dorothea to accompany him.

SERA had never hired a photographer before. It wasn't in the budget and couldn't be done. "A way would have to be found and a way was found," said Dorothea. "My papers were made out as a typist because they'd just roar back if you mentioned photographer."

Dorothea took the boys to stay with a family across the bay in El Cerrito. She and Paul went out in the field, first to the Nipomo pea fields, and then down to the Imperial Valley. They were on the road by six in the morning and went all day, often without stopping to eat or rest. Everywhere they traveled they found the bewildered, drifting migrants.

While Paul interviewed people, Dorothea photographed. Soon she was asking questions herself. After a few minutes she would slip over to Paul and repeat what she had heard, and he would jot it down in his black notebook. Later, she began writing their words down herself.

"The words that come direct from the people are the greatest," Dorothea said.

Family on the Road, San Joaquin Valley, California, 1935

She began keeping a notebook in her car. After getting information from the migrants, she would rush back to the car, holding on to the words with great excitement. She was just hoping she could remember them till she could write them down. She knew that "if you substitute one out of your own vocabulary, it disappears before your eyes."

"This life is simplicity, boiled down," one man told her as he leaned up against his car. "These children of mine would like to be scared to death if they saw a piece of meat in the house," another said.

On a trip in early spring, on a wet, rainy day, Dorothea pulled into a gas station and watched the family at the pump before her.

> *They looked very woebegone to me. They were American whites. I looked at the license plate on the car and it was Oklahoma. I got out and asked which way were they going, were they looking for work? And they said, "We've been blown out." I questioned what they meant, and they told me about the dust storm. They were the first arrivals that I saw. These were the people who got up that day quick and left. They saw they had no crop back there. All of that day, driving for the next three or four hundred miles, I saw these people.*

She was documenting one of the largest migrations of people across the United States. Farmers across the nation were in desperate shape. Crop and livestock prices had plummeted during the Depression, and the use of machines had thrown field hands out of work. Then in 1933 a series of terrible droughts began. Powerful, unrelenting winds and burning heat blew away hundreds of millions of tons of top-soil in enormous dark clouds. Thousands of farms were left desolate. Between 1935 and 1940 more than a million people left their farms and headed for California, hoping to find work in the huge agricultural fields.

When she returned from the field, Dorothea immediately headed for her San Francisco darkroom to develop and print her photographs. Sometimes Paul joined her, eager to see what she had captured on film. He would prepare a written report, detailing the conditions he saw, and recommending that the government build camps. The reports were read in the SERA office, then passed on to the

Bound for California,
Oklahoma, 1938

Federal Emergency Relief Administration in Washington, D.C.

The Taylor-Lange reports were powerfully written, and illustrated with compelling photographs. They made it clear that action was urgently needed. By chance, FERA had $20,000 in its budget for a project that had just been dropped. The money was transferred to SERA to establish the first two emergency California migrant camps. These camps had toilets, hot showers, stoves, tent platforms, a small building for the office manager, and a large community building.

All that spring, Dorothea and Paul continued to drive up and down California, interviewing and photographing the migrants. More and more of Dorothea's time was spent with Paul. She found him deeply attractive, with many characteristics that the temperamental Maynard didn't have. Paul was steady, warm, kind, and loyal. He was also profoundly committed to making a difference in people's lives. Dorothea's marriage, so long in trouble, finally foundered under the strength of her feelings for Paul.

Late in the spring, on a trip through the Imperial Valley, Paul and Dorothea stopped by the side of the road to rest. They walked out into a field that was knee-deep in purple and blue lupine flowers. Neither said a word. Dorothea knew—just from the look that passed between them—that she would spend the rest of her life with Paul.

Dorothea in the Field, 1938 (Photograph by Ron Partridge)

CHAPTER SIX

SLIDING IN ON THE EDGES

"You didn't ever quit in the middle of anything because it was uncomfortable."

In Washington, D.C., the Taylor-Lange reports were seen by Roy Stryker at the Resettlement Administration. Later renamed the Farm Security Administration, or FSA, this office was set up to help rural people all over the United States. Stryker was in charge of letting Americans know how desperate farmers across America were, and why they needed government help. Stryker felt that if the public saw pictures of people in trouble, they would want the government to step in and help. He made sure the FSA photographs were used in newspapers and magazines across the country, as well as seen by politicians.

Stryker found Dorothea's work so revealing he put her on his payroll in August 1935. She joined Arthur Rothstein and Ben Shahn as a staff photographer. The FSA photographers over the next few years included Margaret Bourke-White, Walker Evans, and Russell Lee. From 1935 through 1943, they photographed across America, compiling more than 270,000 photographs.

Shortly after being hired by Stryker, Dorothea went on her first trip for the FSA. She drove north to Marysville, California, and photographed the new migrant camp that the Taylor-Lange reports had helped establish. When she returned home, Stryker asked her to print up some of her earlier work for SERA and send it to him. Eager to have her work seen, she got busy in the darkroom immediately. In three weeks she mailed him fifty prints.

Dorothea waited impatiently for authorization from Stryker to go out in the field again, but he was slow in sending her on another assignment. While she waited, her divorce from Maynard was finalized in November.

On December 6, 1935, Paul and Dorothea were married in Albuquerque, New Mexico. On the afternoon of the same day she went out and photographed. "Our work went on from then, together," said Paul.

But it wasn't always that simple. Out in the field, they were a team, both with equal jobs. But Paul, like Dorothea, had already been married when they fell in love, and he brought three children with him into the marriage: Katherine, thirteen; Ross, ten; and Margot, six. After the divorce, Paul's first wife went back to New York to study psychology, leaving the children with him. Dorothea had full custody of her sons—Dan, now ten, and John, seven.

Ross Taylor, Driven and Angry, 1935

Ready to devote herself to working in the field, Dorothea closed her portrait studio in San Francisco with no regrets. She and Paul rented a house in Berkeley big enough to hold all five children. The house was large and rambling, with windows and doors opening onto a relaxed garden that plunged down to the bottom of the lot.

The children invented a game called "In and Out." Sneaking in and out of the house through any opening possible, one group would defend the house while the other attacked. The game was a neighborhood favorite until one boy, trying for a new exit, got stuck in the chimney and "In and Out" was forbidden.

Dorothea set the household rules and expected them to be followed without complaint. The children weren't allowed to disagree or even question her. Behind

56

her back they called her "Dictator Dot." Paul didn't intervene even when his own children were concerned. He felt she was capable of managing everything, and they both assumed it was her responsibility. "She was harnessed to the house," Paul admitted later. "She was not a liberated woman."

Dorothea made sure the house was immaculate, the wooden floors shining with fresh wax, dishes put away, beds made every morning. Navaho rugs from Maynard lay across the back of the couch, and in the kitchen, copper kettles glowed a deep, burnished brown. In the spring Dorothea brought in tall branches of flowering fruit trees and set them in big earthenware pots throughout the house.

The one place where Dorothea relaxed was in the kitchen. Something about her softened when she prepared food. She was an excellent cook and made rich macaroni and cheese, boiled tongue with green olives, and savory onion soup. In the fall she made marmalades and jellies, then arranged the jars on the window ledge so the light filtered through the deep oranges, pale pinks, and tawny yellows.

Besides gaining three new siblings, there was something else new for Dan and John. Paul, deeply in love with Dorothea, gave his heart to her completely. Dan and John had only faint memories of a house filled with love. Now they had a home, and two adults who loved each other.

During the school year, Paul couldn't always go with Dorothea on her field trips because of his teaching schedule. But she needed help with her heavy equipment and with the driving. And when she returned from the field, she realized she could use an assistant in the darkroom. Imogen's son Ron, now seventeen, jumped at the chance.

The first thing Ron did was to

Ron Partridge, 1939

help build a darkroom in the basement of Dorothea's new house in Berkeley, with a door opening onto the lower garden. When they returned from a trip, they would go straight to the darkroom to develop her film. It was easy to lose track of time in the warm, pungent-smelling darkroom. Sometimes Ron would stay for hours after Dorothea went to bed, developing the film and hanging it up to dry. When he would finally leave, the streetcars had sometimes stopped running for the night. Rather than go back into the house and risk disturbing everyone, Ron would curl up in a pile of leaves in the garden, or walk to a nearby warehouse and sleep on the packing pads till dawn, when he would return to her darkroom.

When they set out to photograph in the field, Ron took the wheel of the old Ford as they roamed up and down California. "I don't think we ever drove more than forty miles in a day," he said. "I'd be going twenty miles an hour and she'd say,

Ron Partridge Photographing at Hooverville, 1939

'Slow down, Ron, slow down.' Her eyes would go from one side to another, taking in every little thing. When we saw something—a broken car, a camp of migrants, a farm machine, a field boss—we would stop."

Gaining the trust of the migrant workers was the first thing Dorothea had to do. That took time. "So often it's just sticking around and remaining there, not swooping in and swooping out in a cloud of dust," explained Dorothea. She would sit down on the ground with people and let the children touch her camera "with their dirty, grimy little hands. You let them because you know that if you behave in a generous manner, you're very apt to receive it. I have asked for a drink of water and taken a long time to drink it, and I have told everything about myself long before I asked any questions."

The migrant workers took her limp into account when they sized her up. They realized immediately that she had dealt with adversity herself, and they were kinder to her. "It gets you off on a different level than if you go into a situation whole and secure," Dorothea explained. "My lameness as a child and acceptance, finally, of my lameness, truly opened gates for me."

When people were comfortable with her, Dorothea began photographing. She often started with the inquisitive children who clustered around her. She worked with a Rolliflex and a 4-by-5 Graflex. The Graflex was large, cumbersome, and heavy. She moved slowly, and waited patiently for just the right moment to take a picture. After each shot, she had to stop and reload the negative holder.

Other photographers were using the new 35 mm cameras, which were small and light and allowed for thirty-six photographs to be taken before reloading the film. But Dorothea wasn't interested in speed. The new cameras didn't suit her working style. "Dorothea really believed that if you photographed someone aggressively, you stole their spirit," Ron explained. "She felt they should be part and parcel of the photographic process."

Usually the migrant workers were eager to cooperate. Dorothea told them the government wanted a record of what was happening so they could help. It meant a lot that the government in far-off Washington cared enough about their troubles to send a photographer.

"We found our way in, slid in on the edges," said Dorothea. "It was hard, hard living. It was rather rough, not too far away from the people we were working

People Living in Miserable Poverty, Shacktown, Oklahoma, 1936

with. We had better food, and we slept in better beds, but you didn't ever quit in the middle of anything because it was uncomfortable."

Sometimes unexpected people turned out to be the most revealing. "The people who are garrulous and wear their heart on their sleeve and tell you everything, that's one kind of person," Dorothea noted. "But the fellow who's hiding behind a tree, and hoping you don't see him, is the fellow that you'd better find out why."

The migrant workers settled into shantytowns, clustered by the side of a river, near an irrigation ditch or pond, or under a highway overpass. People stayed in places where they wouldn't get run off, next to a stream or pond to draw water from. The shantytowns often looked like dumps because the shelters were made of brush, old cardboard, wooden boxes, and cast-off tin roofing.

The camps were crowded and filthy. There wasn't enough food, and what they had was often awful. Sometimes the migrants bathed in the same spot they drew

Child of a Migratory Worker, San Joaquin Valley, California, 1936

Sick Migrant Child, Washington, 1939

their drinking water from. Often there were no bathrooms, so people relieved themselves in the surrounding fields. Flies, moving from the waste in the fields to the camps, spread dysentery, and the children had diarrhea. Epidemics of scarlet fever and typhoid broke out. Even mumps, measles, or whooping cough could kill the weakened, hungry children.

Outside their shelters the families set up stoves. If they were lucky, they still had ham brought from home in old lard cans, and cornmeal for corn bread. There was no milk, not even for the young children, no butter for anyone. If the migrants had enough money, they bought potatoes and cabbage and boiled them. Many meals were simply beans and biscuits, or oatmeal mush.

Ron remembered one Thanksgiving when he and Dorothea were invited into a tent as the family ate dinner. "Each child got a homemade biscuit on their tin plate. White gravy was spooned over it—that's just flour and lard and water cooked together. Then the family bowed their heads and said Grace. 'Thank you God for this food which sustains us.'" Ron and Dorothea found their gratitude unbearably painful. "It broke our hearts, standing there watching them give thanks for so little. We stumbled out of there without even photographing."

But no matter how tough the situation, Dorothea never gave handouts to the migrants. "The only way to really make a difference," she told Ron, "is to let them know in Washington what's going on out here."

After a long day in the field, they would find a room in a cheap auto court. They had to live on four dollars a day, which didn't go far. They stayed in dilapidated old motels with cracked linoleum, one rickety bed, and often no hot water. If the weather was decent, Ron slept outside in his sleeping bag.

One evening they went into one of the higher quality places to register. Dorothea was in her early forties and Ron was only eighteen. The clerk's eyebrows arched up as he stared at this older woman and the young man she had in tow. "Dorothea just looked at him," Ron said, "and she took the pen and wrote down, 'Dorothea Lange and Fancy Man'! Then we walked to the motel room."

Dorothea Being Shown How to Tie on a Potato Sack, 1937

Dorothea Digging Potatoes, 1937 (Photographs by Ron Partridge)

CHAPTER SEVEN

HARDSHIP IN THE FIELDS

*"I have a very great instinct for freedom.
Anybody cuts into that and I churn."*

Dorothea stayed in touch with Stryker at the FSA primarily through letters. Long distance phone calls were expensive and considered a luxury. She wrote to him about how her trips were going, often pleading for more funds for equipment or supplies. Stryker wrote back, telling her what he was looking for, encouraging her, and sending her on new assignments.

In February 1936 Stryker sent her authorization for a month of travel. He closed his letter by saying, "Best wishes for a successful trip, and I hope the cops don't pick you up. Don't let them break your camera."

The agricultural farms Dorothea was photographing were enormous—often hundreds of acres—and belonged to wealthy land owners. Farming in California was "agribusiness." When it was time for planting and harvesting, large influxes of laborers were needed at just the right time. On a farm that had huge peach orchards, for example, it might take two hundred workers to tend to the trees all year round. But at harvest time, two thousand workers would be needed to pick the peaches and box them for shipping.

If the workers didn't show up, or were delayed for some reason, the entire crop would rot in the fields. The owners developed a surefire technique for getting plenty of workers. They sent out advertising circulars to the dust bowl states and ran advertisements in the newspapers that read PLENTY OF WORK! and HIGH WAGES!

In the California camps, word spread quickly about which crops were ripening,

Children of Carrot Pickers, California, 1937

and where. Families packed up their cars and hurried down the highways to be the first hired. When they arrived, they found the wages were terrible. But if one person didn't take the job, hundreds more were pouring into the area who would, just to keep from starving. "The growers offered thirty-five cents an hour for plums and nectarines, twenty cents for potatoes and lettuce, and a starvation pay of two and a half cents for a box of peaches—*one dollar* for a *ton* of peaches."

Out in the fields, Dorothea turned her camera on the children working along-side their parents. They got up early and worked outside in the flat, sun-scorched fields all day. It didn't matter if they were hungry, or even sick. Nobody got to rest.

The family needed food for their next meal and gas for the car so they could make it to the next job.

If the family could get by on the parents' income they would send the children to the local school. Parents knew that migrant work was a dead-end life. If their kids didn't get an education, what would become of them? The children might be in one school for a week or two, or, if they were lucky, for a whole month.

One migrant father described what it felt like to send his children off to school:

> *Picture how you would feel with two or three children headed for school, almost barefoot, with ragged or ill-fitting clothing. You see them going down the road with a paper bag in their hands, with two baking-powder biscuits, maybe, and some beans in between. And if you were a little child, how would you feel going to school that way—and when it comes noon you sit down in your little bunch and drag out those two sandwiches full of beans, when the rest of the little ones are sitting around you there, children of more fortunate people. How do the children feel? How would you feel?*

Girls of Lincoln Bench School, Oregon, 1939

The few camps established by the government gave the migrants a chance at a better life. By paying a dollar a week, they could clean up, wash their clothes, and socialize together in the recreation hall. The tents protected them from the wind and rain and sun. Children were fed breakfast every day for a penny. If the family had no money, they were allowed to work around the camp in exchange for the services they received.

FSA Camp for Migrant Workers, Arvin, California, 1936

The men who owned and ran the huge California farms were adamantly against the government setting up more migrant camps. They were afraid bringing the migrant workers together in large groups, with a recreation hall to meet in, would help them organize and demand better working conditions and higher pay. Local townspeople had their own objections to the camps. They didn't want migrants going to school with their kids, using up the funds in their county relief programs, and getting free medical care at their hospitals.

Dorothea and Paul crusaded tirelessly for the camp program over the next few years. Besides photographing in the fields and filing reports, Dorothea brought her images to newspapers such as the *San Francisco News*, urging them to run articles on the migrant families' plight. When Paul wasn't teaching classes at the university, he talked to community leaders and gave speeches to interested groups. Everywhere he went, he used Dorothea's photographs to illustrate his point.

As the situation got worse, Dorothea asked Stryker to let her photograph in the Imperial Valley. "The region is swamped with moving, homeless families," she wrote. "The people continue to pour in and there is no way to stop them and no work when they get there."

The local government in the Imperial Valley decided to set up a camp for the migrants. "Those in control are bitterly opposed and there is trouble ahead," wrote Dorothea. "If they don't like you they shoot at you. Beat you up and throw you into a ditch at the county line." Despite the violence, Dorothea went with her camera and returned home unharmed.

One of the most successful government camps she photographed was Shafter Camp, run by a man named Tom Collins. He was a "slim, dark, wiry, nervous fellow who studied that camp and camp life like no other camp manager." Every day he flew the American flag over the camp, and he was fiercely protective of the people living there.

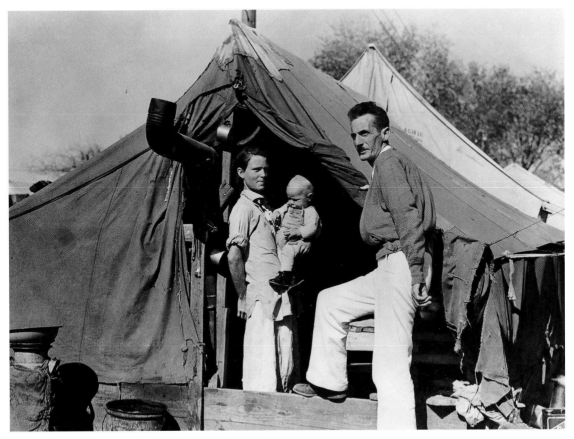

Tom Collins and Migrant Family, Shafter, California, 1936

Writer John Steinbeck met Tom Collins, and the two traveled together in a used bakery truck they called "the old pie wagon." Steinbeck, a native Californian, was deeply concerned about the migratory families.

In February 1938 the FSA asked Steinbeck to write about the conditions he saw. Steinbeck went out in the fields when heavy rains had been falling for three weeks. He wrote a friend that thousands of migrants families were "starving to death . . . not just hungry, but actually starving. The government is trying to feed them and get medical attention to them with the . . . banks and huge growers sabotaging the thing all along the line and yelling for a balanced budget. I'm going to break the story hard enough so that food and drugs can get moving." A month later Steinbeck was back in the fields, refusing to take any money for his work. "The suffering is too great for me to cash in on it," he wrote. "The water is a foot

Oklahoma Child with Cotton Sack Ready to Go into the Field, 7 A.M., California, 1936

Hop Harvesting, Oregon, 1939
"This boy, age 11, and his grandmother work side by side picking hops. Started work at 5 A.M. Photograph was made at noon.
Temperature 105."

Girl Carrying Full Cotton Sack, California, 1936

deep in the tents and the children are up on their beds and there is no food. . . . It is the most heartbreaking thing in the world. I want to put a tag of shame on the greedy bastards who are responsible for this."

To raise money for the migrants, a group put together a pamphlet called "Their Blood Is Strong," using Steinbeck's newspaper articles and Dorothea's photographs. It sold for twenty-five cents and was reprinted four times. But it was Steinbeck's book *The Grapes of Wrath*, published in the spring of 1939, that truly shocked

Americans by revealing the terrible conditions of the migrant workers.

Responding to public pressure, the government established over twenty-five camps. Never enough to house all the migrants, they at least provided places of respite for some of the weary field-workers.

Over the next few years, letters between Stryker and Dorothea became more tense. Though they thought highly of each other, both were stubborn and irritable when crossed. Stryker insisted on doing things his way. Dorothea had her own ideas and refused to follow all of his instructions. "I have a very great instinct for freedom," she said. "Anybody cuts into that and I churn."

Dorothea nearly wore herself out working for the FSA. When she returned home from the fields she needed her home to be a calm and peaceful retreat where she could rest and enjoy being with her family. But after several years of "Dictator Dot," the children, now teenagers, were uncooperative. They were tired of Dorothea's formidable will controlling their lives.

John and his friends prowled the neighborhood, getting into mischief. When the fraternity houses at the university had outdoor parties, the boys wriggled into the bushes and used peashooters to shoot out the lights and hit the students with hard, dry peas. They soaped the streetcar tracks so that the streetcars spun their wheels helplessly as they headed up the steep hills, then slid back down.

Dan rebelled more forcefully against his mother's rigid rules. He began staying out late, refusing to say where he was. Around Dorothea and Paul he was angry and sullen. Every time they pulled him out of a new scrape, Paul would sit down with Dan for a talk, hoping to straighten him out. "I am prepared," Paul would always end, "to try again."

Paul also talked with John. "We can't have more than one person upsetting your mother," he warned. John could see that Dorothea was exhausted and anxious. He didn't want to make things worse, so he "stuffed himself away," acting compliant and easygoing.

Kathy and Margot went to live with their mother. Ross retreated to his room, practicing the French horn for hours on end. He had a natural gift for music, and there was no doubt he would someday be a brilliant French horn player. But the stress of work and home continued to wear down Dorothea. She began suffering from bad stomach pains.

Dorothea with Zeiss Jewell Camera, 1937 (Photograph by Ron Partridge)

CHAPTER EIGHT

THE SOUTH

"One should really use the camera as though tomorrow you'd be stricken blind."

Whaen Dorothea first worked for the FSA, she concentrated her efforts on the West Coast, traveling mostly in California, but also going up into Oregon, Washington, and Idaho. But the West Coast wasn't the only place feeling the effects of the Depression.

Wanting to see conditions in more of America, Dorothea boarded the children out with other families or sent them to summer camp during the summers of 1937, 1938, and 1939. She and Paul took long trips through the Southwest and into the South. Driving thousands of miles on hot, dusty, back country roads, Dorothea photographed teenagers walking barefoot behind tired mules, men perched high up on tractors, and children filling large cotton sacks with wriggling boll weevils they had plucked off the cotton plants.

She and Paul were fascinated by the differences between the restless, moving migrants, searching for a home, and the rooted, traditional society they found in the South. "Earlier, I'd gotten at people through the ways they had been torn loose," Dorothea said. "Now I had to get at them through the ways they were bound up."

Farm Boy with a Sack Full of Boll Weevils, Georgia, 1937

75

She struggled to capture the relationships of the old plantation owners to the workers, the farmers to the soil, the mule giving way to the tractor. She found people living in a system where the southern landowners, often the descendents of the original owners of the plantations, allowed people to live on their land and grow crops. The tenants, called sharecroppers, gave the owners part of their harvest every year. The impoverished sharecroppers often had to borrow ahead from the owners to buy food, seed, and farm animals. Some years they didn't make enough money to pay back what they had borrowed. They were caught in a terrible cycle of debt and poverty.

The land, long farmed in just cotton, was worn out. Sharecroppers, both black and white, were less and less able to make a living. Erosion, the boll weevil, and a poor market for cotton devastated landowners and left hungry families on used-up land.

Everywhere Dorothea went she saw the introduction of the tractor creating

Father and Son on a Tractor, Texas, 1938

Thirteen-Year-Old Sharecropper Cultivating a Field, Georgia, 1937

enormous change. It took just one man with a tractor to do the work of eight men with eight mules. All across the South, thousands of sharecroppers were being turned off the land they had farmed for decades, even generations.

When Dorothea got back to California she rushed into the darkroom, worried that the relentless, muggy heat of the South might have ruined her film. To her immense relief, her film was fine. But what bothered her, as always, was the content of the images. She made prints and pinned them up on the living room wall. Standing back, she looked them over with a critical eye. "Not good enough, Dorothea, not good enough," she muttered to herself. She wrote Stryker, "I wish

Young Sharecropper and His First Child, North Carolina, 1939

that I could work the whole trip over again, go to the same places—knowing what I know now—but then I always wish that in this kind of work."

A letter from Stryker in the fall of 1939 warned Dorothea that her job was in danger. The FSA was being threatened with huge budget cuts. Stryker didn't know how severe the cuts would be.

While Stryker was informing Dorothea of his budget problems, she was begging to be sent out in the field again. She wrote to tell him that a strike was going on in the lettuce fields around Salinas and she wanted to go photograph. But in late fall, Stryker wrote Dorothea to tell her she would be dropped from the payroll on January 1, 1940.

Both Dorothea and Paul were deeply hurt. Though Stryker said it was not personal, it was well known he found Dorothea demanding and impossible. A friend

Waterboy, Mississippi Delta, 1938

of Paul and Dorothea's, Jonathan Garst, wrote to Stryker, hoping to heal the breach. He reminded Stryker how much Dorothea and Paul had done for migrant workers and the camp program, and how Paul had devoted his life to the problems of the rural poor. Jonathan closed by saying, "Moreover, Paul Taylor is apparently still violently in love with Dorothea Lange and takes her problems very much to heart." But the appeal made no difference, and Dorothea was not reinstated.

All across America, people's focus was shifting away from the Depression. World War II was raging in Europe, and Americans watched with horror as European countries, one by one, fell under Hitler's rule.

The war in far-off Europe and losing her job were not Dorothea's only concerns. At home, Dan was increasingly angry and rebellious. He dropped out of high school, ill-adjusted and unhappy. One day in a wild act of defiance Dan stole her camera, sold it to a hockshop, and ran away from home.

Dorothea and Paul tracked him down in San Francisco. Though furious and hurt, Dorothea was also deeply worried. She urged Dan to come home. Paul, quiet and thoughtful, extended a hand to his stepson. "I am prepared," Paul said gravely, "to try again."

Dorothea Lange Photographing the Japanese-American Evacuation, 1942 (Photographer unknown)

CHAPTER NINE

JAPANESE AMERICAN INTERNMENT

"This is what we did. How did it happen? How could we?"

John was playing in a park near his house when an older boy ran by him yelling, "The Japanese bombed Pearl Harbor!" John rushed home to tell Dorothea and Paul.

Early that morning, December 7, 1941, the Imperial Japanese forces had bombed Pearl Harbor, a U.S. naval base in Hawaii. Up to that moment, Americans had been conflicted about entering World War II. Some Americans urged the president to join the Allies in fighting Hitler in Europe, while others wanted to stay out of the war entirely. The shock of the bombing drew Americans together overnight, and President Roosevelt declared war on Japan and her allies, Germany and Italy.

The Japanese military moved quickly, winning a series of stunning victories in the Pacific. By February 15, 1942, they had captured Guam, Hong Kong, Manila, and Singapore.

With every Japanese victory, anti-Japanese hysteria increased in America. People were afraid Japan would attack the West Coast. They thought that large numbers of Japanese and Japanese Americans living on the West Coast would help the Japanese to overrun the United States. A San Francisco newspaper columnist wrote, "I am for immediate removal of every Japanese on the West Coast. Herd 'em up, pack 'em off. Let 'em be pinched, hurt and hungry!"

The Japanese living in America, and their children, Japanese Americans, were profoundly loyal Americans. These Nikkei (pronounced neek-kay) immediately

High School Boys Before Evacuation, San Francisco, 1942

made an effort to prove their patriotism. Many Nikkei burnt their family photographs of kimono-clad relatives, destroyed books written in Japanese, and threw out their beautiful ceremonial kimonos and Samurai swords. The five thousand Japanese Americans who were in the military at the time of Pearl Harbor continued to serve. The Japanese American Citizens' League sent a telegram to President Roosevelt saying, "We are ready and prepared to expend every effort to repel this invasion together with our fellow Americans."

But their efforts made no difference. On February 19, 1942, Roosevelt issued Executive Order 9066. He called for the forcible removal of all people of Japanese descent living on the West Coast. The Nikkei were to go to "relocation centers" for the duration of the war. These centers were set up in desolate, far-away places with barrack-like housing surrounded by high barbed wire fences, tall towers, searchlights, and armed guards.

Dorothea was asked to photograph this process by the War Relocation Authority (WRA). She took the job but felt terribly conflicted about it. Most Americans supported the president's decision. But Dorothea and Paul were devastated by Executive Order 9066. The Nikkei had committed no crimes, broken no laws, had no trials. Yet they were being imprisoned. Though popularly referred to as an internment, it was legally an incarceration. Overnight the government snatched away the Nikkei's civil liberties—basic freedoms so important that they were guaranteed to all Americans by the Bill of Rights.

Dorothea and Paul were shocked that the government was locking up the Nikkei, two-thirds of whom were American citizens. Even though we were at war with Germany and Italy as well, we weren't locking up Americans of German and Italian ancestry. Dorothea was sure that racial prejudice and hysteria played a part in Roosevelt's order. The best she could do was to photograph the process, so

Children at Raphael Weill Public School Before the Evacuation, San Francisco, 1942

there would be a clear record of what was actually happening. Ron had joined the navy, so she took a new assistant, Chrissie Gardner.

Each Nikkei family was assigned a number and told to prepare for departure in seven days. They had to store or get rid of their cars, rent or sell their houses, close down their businesses, and leave their farms. They set off with a few belongings packed into boxes and suitcases, not knowing how they were going to be treated.

During this time, Dorothea photographed the Nikkei in their homes, on their farms, and at school. In a strawberry field near Sacramento, California, she photographed a young soldier who had been furloughed from the army to help his mother and family prepare for the evacuation.

Preparing for Evacuation, Sacramento County, California, May 1942

Mochida Family Awaiting Evacuation Bus, 1942

"Evacuation tags are used to keep the family intact during the evacuation. Mochida opened a nursery and five greenhouses on a two acre site. He raised snapdragons and sweetpeas."

Getting on Evacuation Bus, Centerville, California, 1942

Dorothea and Chrissie went to the bus and train stations to photograph the Nikkei as they were being shipped out to temporary "assembly centers." An unnatural quiet hung over the stations. Everyone seemed totally stunned. They sat waiting for hours on suitcases and bags, or stood in long lines to be checked in by the military police. Dorothea was always viewed with suspicion, her credentials checked time and again. "Who is this woman?" the military police would demand. "What is she doing with a camera?"

She followed the Nikkei to Tanforan, a Bay Area racetrack, where some families were housed in horse stalls that had been hastily swept out. Straw and horse dung filled the corners, and the smell of urine and manure hung in the air. The new inhabitants quickly got busy with soap and water, cleaning out their quarters. That night, everyone was given an army cot to sleep on and an empty sack to stuff with straw for a mattress.

Several months later the Nikkei were sent to permanent centers. Dorothea made three trips to one of the California centers, Manzanar, in the Owens Valley. Large extended families were housed in cramped barracks. They waited in long lines to eat in the communal mess hall. Each large shower and toilet facility was shared by 250 people. Down the middle of the cement floor a double row of toilets ran back to back with no partitions.

The camp was in the middle of a bleak, windblown desert. In the springtime the wind would tear through the camp, engulfing people in swirling masses of sand and dust. The winter rains turned the dust into heavy, cloying mud. The barracks had only thin tar paper covering the boards to keep out the weather.

Manzanar Relocation Center, 1942

Sixth-Grade Students Studying at the Volunteer Elementary School, Manzanar, 1942

Though the Nikkei were not in physical danger, it was a difficult and humiliating time emotionally. Families struggled to remain strong, and to manage with so little privacy.

Parents were worried about their children missing school, and impromptu classes were immediately set up. At first there were no classrooms or desks for the students. After school and on weekends they gathered in the wide open spaces of Manzanar and played baseball until the gathering darkness forced them indoors.

Over time, the Nikkei organized newspapers, churches, libraries, and hospitals. For the children there were many activities, such as Scout troops, baton twirling contests, art classes, and dances for the teenagers. But no one ever forgot that the boundary of their community was a barbed wire fence.

After one particularly strenuous day of photographing, Dorothea lay flat on her bed, totally exhausted, with terrible burning pains in her stomach. The haunting, desolate camp affected her deeply. She was horrified that the government could lock people up "completely on the basis of what blood may be coursing through a person's veins, nothing else. Nothing to do with your affiliations or friendships or associations. Just blood."

Dorothea was consumed with fear over what she dreaded. If the government could take away the civil liberties of this group of people, who would be next? Which of the freedoms Americans took for granted might also be taken away? Her core belief in the fairness and strength of democracy was shaken.

Her stomach problems increased, sapping her strength. Dorothea was not able to work as she would have liked. "World in agony, camera dusty," she jotted on a piece of paper. "Some work accomplished, not organized or well built. Much energy lost, no drive. Busyness, frustration. Paul my haven, my love. My anchor."

Though the government considered the Nikkei dangerous enough to lock up, they did recruit young Japanese Americans from the camps to serve in the armed forces. More than 3,500 served in the Pacific, and the 442 Regimental Combat team, fighting in Europe and North Africa, became the most decorated American unit in the war.

In December 1944, the United States Supreme Court ruled that Japanese American citizens who were loyal could not be kept in camps or off the West Coast. All the camps except one were closed down by December 1945, and almost all the Nikkei released.

Paul and Dorothea did what they could to help. Paul served as vice chairman of the Pacific Coast Committee for American Principles and Fair Play. He urged people to band together and speak out loudly against prejudice toward the home-coming Nikkei.

Sometimes it was a difficult battle. In Placer County, California, a Citizens' Anti-Japanese League formed, stating: "To say it is our duty to civilize, humanize and Christianize the Japs is just bunk. If we must do something for them, let us sterilize them." They didn't want the Nikkei returning to their agricultural community, preferring instead to hire Mexicans and schoolchildren to harvest the crops.

Fortunately, many Americans were more open-minded. But many of the Nikkei had no homes, farms, or businesses to return to. What they had stored had often been vandalized and stolen. Financially destroyed, they had to start all over again.

More than forty years later, the government issued a formal apology and gave twenty thousand dollars to each surviving Japanese American who had been in the camps during the war. It was an important acknowledgment that the government had violated the principles of freedom which are at the core of American democracy.

Dorothea in New Jersey, ca. 1947 (Photograph by Sol Libsohn)

CHAPTER TEN

THE SHIPYARD YEARS

"You can't deny what you must do, no matter what it costs."

A few miles from Dorothea's home in Berkeley were the Richmond shipyards, a small industry where about six thousand people built merchant vessels, freighters, and tankers. When the United States entered World War II, these shipyards expanded almost overnight to meet the tremendous need for warships. Migrant farmworkers turned their backs on the orchards and fields. They were welcomed into high-paying jobs in the Bay Area shipyards. African-Americans threw down their hoes and quit their hardscrabble lives by the thousands. California held out new promise. One African-American woman said, "The war made me live better, it really did. My sister always said that Hitler got us out of the white folks' kitchen."

By 1944 the Bay Area had the biggest shipbuilding industry in the world, employing more than 240,000 people. The "yards" operated around the clock. Three shifts of workers kept the ship production moving at a staggering pace.

Dorothea teamed up with Ansel Adams to photograph the shipyards for *Fortune* magazine. They were an unlikely pair. Ansel drove up in his station wagon loaded with equipment and set up a tripod, big lights, and a platform to photograph from. He had a huge, bushy beard and a ten-gallon hat. Crowds gathered to watch him. Dorothea picked up her camera, slipped her notebook and some extra film into her pocket, and melted into the crowd. Ansel captured the grand, wide view of the environment, and Dorothea caught the small, telling aspects of the workers' lives.

In the shipyards, tens of thousands of women were doing "men's" jobs. They operated all kinds of heavy equipment—welding torches, drill presses, riveting guns, and tall cranes.

It was an exciting time for the newly employed women. They were helping their country in the war effort as well as earning money. But during the whole war, only one woman was promoted to foreman. Men didn't mind working with women, but they didn't want to work under them.

Martin, Dorothea's brother, got a job as a foreman in the yards. Because he was always on the move, cajoling, urging, pushing his workers to work faster, he was nicknamed "Walkin' Marty Lange." Martin got Dan a job on his crew. Dan worked alongside Martin until, one day, he decided he had had enough. Without giving notice, he quit.

Dorothea despaired of Dan ever getting on his feet. She didn't know how to help. Paul thought the army might straighten him out, and urged him to enlist. Dan joined the army, but he went AWOL so often he was in the stockade more often than not.

Besides photographing in the yards, Dorothea took her camera into the nearby towns. She wanted to show how people lived while working in the yards. She found the streets bustling with activity. Stores and movie theaters stayed open around the clock to

Welder, Richmond Shipyards, California, 1943

Shipyard Workers Children at Window, Richmond, California, 1943

accommodate workers. Many schools operated in two shifts, with sixty kids to a classroom. Where were all these families living? How were they living?

The government built twenty-five thousand new housing units near the shipyards, but still people scrambled to find a place to stay. Whole families lived in small trailers, garages, converted chicken coops, and old water towers. Sometimes two workers shared a single bed, one sleeping while the other worked.

For many of the children, life was much better in the Bay Area. The former migrant kids could stay in school, instead of moving from school to school as they followed the crops, or dropping out altogether. The African-American children weren't segregated into substandard schools separate from the white children.

Dorothea visited one school with her camera and asked the question: "How many of you were *not* born in California?" Nearly all the children raised their hands.

Because the adults were making good wages, there were often opportunities for

Richmond School Children—Every Hand Up Signifies a Child Not Born in California, 1942

kids to earn a little money as well. They could sell newspapers, work in a store after school, or baby-sit younger children while their parents worked in the yards.

Despite her stomach pain, Dorothea was determined to make a record of the tremendous social changes going on around her. "You can't deny what you must do, no matter what it costs. And with me it was always expenditure to the last ditch. I know the last ditch. I've lived on the last ditch."

Lunch Break, Richmond Shipyards, California, 1943

Her doctor gently suggested she take it easy. "Take it easy?" she replied irritably. "How can a photographer take it easy?"

The month the war ended, August 1945, Dorothea's health gave out completely. She had her gall bladder removed, but the surgery only made things worse. Bleeding heavily, she was rushed back to the hospital. "It was a terrible time," her husband Paul said. "We thought we had lost her." She recovered, only to be told she needed to go back to the hospital in 1946.

Dorothea was at her doctor's office getting ready for surgery when the phone rang. The doctor answered it. "It's for you," he said, handing it to Dorothea. It was her son Dan. "Dad is dead," he said and hung up.

"I'm sorry," Dorothea said to the doctor. "I've got to go home." After years of struggling for every breath, Maynard's lungs had finally given out, and he died at the age of seventy-one.

Dorothea and Paul, Utah, 1953 (Photograph by Ansel Adams)

CHAPTER ELEVEN

WORLD TRAVELS

*"Now, at a time when I have such feeble energies,
I could do my best work, I know."*

A short time later Dorothea went back to the hospital for surgery, another in an endless cycle of hospital and doctor visits that would dominate the next ten years of her life. Bouts of severe illness were followed by long periods of time when she was confined to home, working quietly in her garden, cooking and sewing.

Sometimes Dorothea despaired of ever using a camera again. "This is the simple fact," she wrote in her journal. "I endure pain a part of every day. This leaves exhaustion. It hurts me. Sometimes, if I am alone, I cry out. Sometimes I am stronger and can endure it."

Anguish over her son Dan made things worse. Discharged from the army, he had returned to Berkeley, living on the streets, sleeping behind houses, and showering at the university gym.

Ron had married and now lived in the country about an hour away. "Let Dan come live here with me," Ron said to Dorothea. "After a few weeks, he'll start working around the place, and he'll do better. The country life will do him good."

Dorothea said no. "He's got to learn to stand on his own two feet," she said to Ron. But when Dan came home there were arguments, anger, and tears. Finally Dorothea and Paul banned him from the house.

Lyde Wall, who lived next door to Dorothea, kept the

Lyde Wall, Northern California, 1944

household running whenever Dorothea had to go back to the hospital. Lyde walked so often between their houses that she wore a deep path in the dirt between their back doors.

As Dorothea's health slowly improved, she went out photographing for a few hours at a time. She bought a 35 mm camera, which was lightweight and easy to carry. At home she began wearing it on a strap around her neck so that she could quickly take a picture if something interested her. And she tore apart her studio, throwing away "mountains of photographic trash" and reorganizing her negatives.

Going over all her work, Dorothea found that her focus was shifting. Earlier, she had photographed people in relation to harsh, powerful events like the Great Depression, the dust bowl, and World War II. Now she was trying to get at something else. She wanted to show people in relation to people, to see what they meant to one another and to themselves. These are "things you have to look very hard to see," said Dorothea, "because they have been taken for granted not only by our eyes, but often by our hearts as well."

One cold, rainy November night Dorothea answered a knock at the back door. Sick, half-starved, Dan stood in the rain, waiting to see what his mother would do. They hadn't seen each other for many months.

Dorothea stared at her son. His clothes were worn and dirty, his face unshaven. His feverish eyes had a pleading, defiant look. "Come in," she said, pulling the door wide open. Dorothea put Dan to bed and took care of him until he was well.

While Dan was gathering his strength, he worked in the garden during the day. He asked his mother if he could write a magazine article about her and use her photos to illustrate it. She agreed, and he spent his evenings writing.

Despite their difficult times, Dan captured her essence in a few succinct sentences. "She is almost mysteriously intuitive, and senses change in her surroundings before she is aware of change in herself. Like lightning, in flashes, she responds to atmosphere, and because her responses are expressed as passionately as they are, the atmosphere responds to her."

The article was accepted, with a payment of five hundred dollars. It was a turning point for Dan. He realized there was something he was good at: writing. He used thirty dollars of his newly earned money to buy a typewriter and wrote another article.

Over the next few years, all of Paul and Dorothea's children married. Margot and Kathy moved back East with their husbands. Ross played the French horn with the San Francisco Symphony, Dan wrote freelance magazine articles, and John became a building contractor. He and his wife Helen, had the first grand-child, Gregor. When John brought the new baby home, Dorothea was ready with her camera. Just as she had photographed John years earlier offering her flowers for Mother's Day, she now photographed him offering his newborn child to the camera, a shy, serious look on his face.

Firstborn, 1952

When John's second son, Andrew, was born, his left arm hung weakly at his side, injured during a long, difficult birth. Dorothea panicked. She thought she had long ago made peace with her limp, but powerful feelings of inadequacy, pain, and anger about her polio came flooding back. She remembered the terrible isolation, the teasing, the admonishment of her mother to "walk as well as you can."

"Everyone else was very brave," Dorothea said later about her grandson's injury. "But I couldn't take it, because I knew. Cripples know that about each other, perfectly well. When I'm with someone that has a disability, we know." With vivid clarity, Dorothea could imagine the painful struggles Andrew had before him.

Her feelings raw and fiercely protective, Dorothea photographed the new baby resting on his mother's lap, her legs strong beneath him, as if she could carry the weight of the world for him.

Helen and Andrew, 1955

John and Helen took their baby to a specialist who taught them a series of exercises to do with him. To Dorothea's enormous relief, Andrew gained nearly normal use of his arm over the next few months.

Though Dorothea was able to do little productive work during the 1950s, interest in her photography was growing. Her images were included in large photography exhibits such as "America's Many Faces," "The Bitter Years," and "The Family of Man." Asked several times to put together a one-woman show, she declined. She didn't think her work was strong enough to carry a whole show.

Now in her early sixties,

Dorothea settled into a quiet life. She and Paul spent weekends at Steep Ravine, a tiny cabin perched on the edge of the Pacific Ocean. When her health permitted, she worked on photo essays, publishing several magazine articles. She and Dan worked on two of them together for *Life* magazine.

No matter what she was doing, Dorothea stopped all work in late November and devoted herself to the holidays. She gathered her family and close friends together for a huge Thanksgiving dinner, and spent the weeks before Christmas decorating the house, choosing perfect presents for everyone, and cooking an enormous dinner. She loved having her whole family gathered together to celebrate the holidays.

❖   ❖   ❖

Early in 1958, Paul was asked to do some consulting work overseas. From his years of studying rural life in America, he had developed a deep interest in how to improve the lives of rural people worldwide. Knowing he would be gone a long time, Paul wanted Dorothea to come with him. Concerned about her health, Dorothea asked her doctor what she should do. "What does it matter if you die here or there?" he said. "Go!"

Over the next several years, Paul and Dorothea traveled first to Asia, then South America and the Middle East. The tremendous impact of Asia overwhelmed Dorothea. The crowded, filthy streets reminded her of her childhood walks along the Bowery in New York City. She found it hard to capture on film "the collision of cultures and people and the teamingness, the noise and the life and the antiquity and the brilliance."

But she kept photographing, taking her camera to familiar places: the marketplace, the fields, the streets, temples and churches. She couldn't talk to people or read the street signs, and she often didn't fully understand what was happening around her. She found herself searching people's faces, looking for universal expressions of pleasure, pain, sorrow, concern, and joy. Gradually people began to stand out as individuals, and she took delicate, tender photographs of them.

On Paul and Dorothea's final trip through the Middle East in 1963, Dorothea's health suddenly plummeted. She was racked with chills and high fevers. No matter what the doctors tried, the fevers came back, ravaging her already weak body.

Schoolroom, Egypt, 1963

"The face is very often a mask. These are unmasked faces."

Family on Street Corner, Ecuador, 1960

Boy in Ecuador, 1960

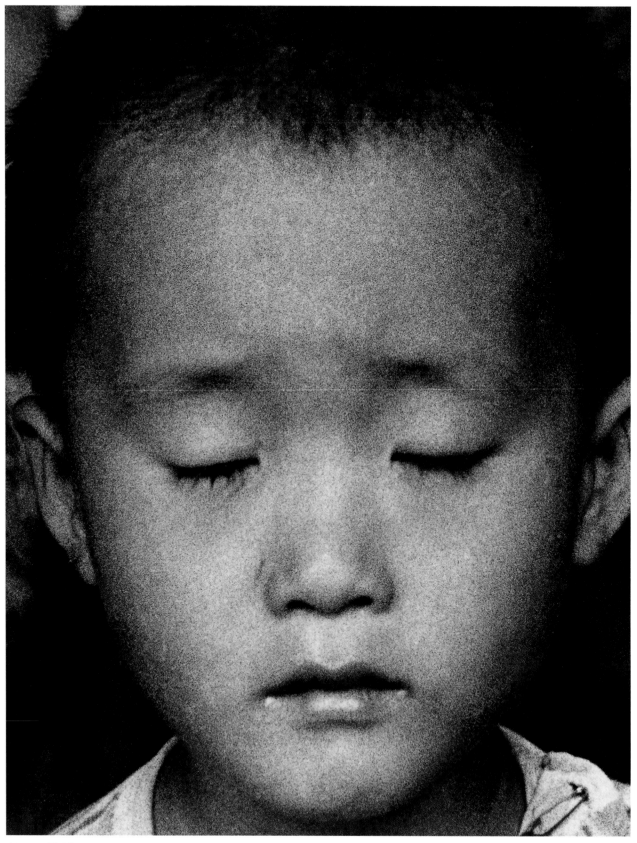

Korean Child, 1958

Unable to eat, she rapidly lost weight and had to use safety pins to hold up her pants. Dorothea was frightened. No one knew what was wrong.

One night in Iran, Paul was awakened by Dorothea thrashing around in bed and muttering incoherently. Her fever had shot up to 103. Paul rushed her onto a plane for Europe, hoping to find more modern medical care.

The European doctors discovered she had malaria and began quinine treatment. For three weeks she stayed in a hospital in Switzerland, slowly improving. Paul and Dorothea spent their days reading and talking quietly, looking out their window at the tidy, well-tended gardens and orchards surrounding the building.

For the first time in many months Dorothea felt peaceful and safe. She asked the Swiss doctor, "If I know when my last illness is, may I come to spend it here?"

"Yes," he replied, "you may."

Her words turned out to be prophetic. Just a year later Dorothea was diagnosed with cancer. Paul wrote to the Swiss doctor, asking if she could return.

Working on the MOMA Show, 1964 (Photograph by Ron Partridge)

CHAPTER TWELVE

THE RIGHT TIME

"The secret places of the heart are the real mainsprings of one's actions."

"In the last two weeks time has stood still," Dorothea wrote to a friend. "I now know that I shall not recover as I have been able to so many times before, for I have an inoperable and incurable cancer of the esophagus, and the way ahead is unchartable."

The doctor in Switzerland said Dorothea was welcome to return to his hospital. Paul and Dorothea talked it over. She longed for the deep peace and gentle care she remembered from Switzerland. But she would have to say good-bye to her family, give up her garden, her darkroom, and her photography. Dorothea wasn't ready to give up.

For several years the Museum of Modern Art in New York had wanted to do a retrospective show, covering her lifetime of photography. With her diagnosis came the sure knowledge that if she didn't put together the show immediately, she would never do it.

"I'm now faced with a really tremendous and dangerous job. I would very much like to avoid it," Dorothea explained. "On the other hand, I feel I must do it." She knew that choosing her best photographs and putting them up on the museum walls would be baring her soul for the world to see.

The museum curator John Szarkowski flew in from New York. Together they began looking over all of Dorothea's photographs. The living room was transformed into a workplace. Dorothea and Szarkowski put up rows of prints on the long white living room wall, discussing and arranging them, taking some away and

Andrew, Berkeley, 1959
"My grandmother told me that of all the things that were beautiful in the world there was nothing finer than an orange. And I've caught myself with my own grandchildren, showing them what a beautiful thing is an eggshell, forgetting where I had gotten that."

adding others. Stacks of photographs were piled up on the tables and chairs as they haggled over which were exactly the right ones.

"In this show, I would like to be speaking to others in the sound of my own voice, poor though it may be," Dorothea insisted. "Not other people's voices. I would put things in that other people wouldn't. I don't care how wide I lay myself open, this time."

Paul Carrying Lisa,
Steep Ravine, 1962

Children Reading, Steep Ravine, 1961 (author in foreground with braids)

One of the most delicate, vulnerable areas Dorothea explored was "Home." In the 1920s, 1930s, and 1940s she had mostly photographed other people's homes, their lack of a home, or their settling down into a new home. But for the last two decades, cut down by her illness, she often photographed close to her own home, taking pictures of her grown children and grandchildren.

But she didn't want to show only the joyful moments of family life. She wanted to weave in trouble and sorrow, in their right place. It was a complex problem she set for herself, though a fitting one. Trouble and sorrow had often shadowed the most tender moments of her family life.

Bad Trouble over the Weekend, 1964

Dorothea worked all spring on the retrospective show. Every morning Paul would serve her breakfast in bed; then she'd come downstairs and work until noon. After a short nap, she'd work again until she was completely wrung out. Throughout the day she'd take tiny bites of custards and Jell-O, and swallow small sips of creamy soups and milk shakes. Gradually the exhibit began to take shape.

The doctor told her she would probably live through the summer, but she must stay on the quiet side. How could she? She still had work to accomplish. "I have not been able to break the habit of thinking everything is ahead," she said. "That has been my lifelong attitude. I find that every day, taken separately, with full weight given to each hour, has seen me through the last months, and in some ways it has been a great time."

When she felt up to it, she and Paul went out to their cabin at Steep Ravine. Here she felt "unlocked and free"—no telephone, no electricity, only the most basic cooking arrangements. Here, Dorothea was loosened from her own critical nature. In their tiny wooden house, buffeted by the salty ocean winds and beat upon by the sun, Paul and Dorothea drew together their scattered children and grandchildren. They'd walk on the beach, climb over the rough coastal rocks, gather driftwood, and dream in front of the fire.

At the end of August, Szarkowski came back to Berkeley and went over the photographs Dorothea wanted to include. He encouraged, cajoled, disagreed, and wrangled with her over her selection. Dorothea often chose photos because of their strong emotional impact, but Szarkowski would swiftly veto them if they were not clean, sharp photos. Together they put together a show that was stronger than either could have done alone.

An old photography friend came to visit in the early fall. It was a bad day for Dorothea, and she was unable to get up. She lay in bed while he talked quietly to her. Suddenly she said, "I just photographed you." He knew what she meant. Unable to hold a camera, she still had been observing him as if she were photographing. Perhaps she was watching how the light fell on his face, the subtle changes in expression as he talked, the soft, rich tones of the background. "To live a visual life is an enormous undertaking," Dorothea said. "I've only touched it, just touched it."

A few weeks later, knowing she was dying, Dorothea had Paul drive her to the hospital. Her daughter-in-law Helen brought in fresh pine branches and lay them on the bed. Dorothea breathed in the sharp, piney scent and smiled. Dan and John sat beside her, each holding one of her hands.

Late that night, alone with Paul, she whispered, "Isn't it a miracle that this comes at the right time!"

Dorothea died just before dawn, on October 11, 1965.

Bitsie and Dorothea, 1961 (Photograph by Ron Partridge)

THANKSGIVING

"Carefully, Bitsie. Carefully."

Dorothea always scared me a little when I was growing up. I was always cautious, a little watchful, when I was with her. She had no tolerance for softness or vagueness, even in children. One Christmas Eve, when I was helping her pass mulled wine to the adults, she put each small, silver cup in my hands with the admonition, "Carefully, Bitsie. Carefully." From Dorothea, this wasn't just a casual or off-hand remark, it was a precisely worded way of being.

And extra carefully I passed the wine to each adult, concentrating fully, not wanting to spill a drop, determined to do right in Dorothea's eyes. I didn't understand that she demanded of those close to her what she demanded of herself—everything.

But even when I was very young I understood that Ron, my father, loved Dorothea in a way that was fierce and intense, part son, part apprentice, part colleague. And Dorothea loved him back, part mother, part teacher, part colleague. For Ron, she wanted a career as a major photographer. She knew he had the talent; what was missing was the drive. One day she took him aside. "Ron," she said, "I think it is time for you to go to New York and become a famous photographer. Leave your wife and children here. Paul and I will take care of them. Devote yourself to photography."

The choice was simple for my father. He stayed. Dorothea forgave him, but always thought it was a weakness in him.

113

One of the most wonderful ways Dorothea filled my childhood was her holiday celebrations. In mid-November she stopped working as a photographer. She unpinned all the photographs from the long, white living room wall and put them away. She tidied her stacks of photographs and papers and shoved them into cabinets, out of sight. From Thanksgiving till after Christmas she stayed out of the darkroom. The holidays were family time for Dorothea, completely and wholeheartedly, with no interruptions from her photographic life allowed.

One Thanksgiving when I was about eleven, my father and mother bundled us five children in the car, just as they had for all the Thanksgivings I could remember, and in the early afternoon we drove across town to Dorothea and Paul's house. Perennially late, we were the last to arrive. We knew that Dan would already be there with his wife Mia and daughter Leslie, as well as John, his wife Helen, and their children, Gregor, Andrew, and Lisa. Ross and his wife Onnie would have already arrived with Dee, Paulie, and Seth. Most likely there would also be friends of Paul and Dorothea's from another country, with unpronounceable names and difficult accents.

We arrived to find the house full of the smells of

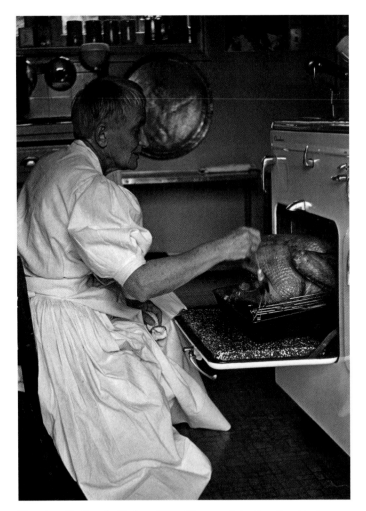

Dorothea Basting the Turkey, 1962 (Photograph by Ron Partridge)

114

dinner cooking, and the family in their festive clothes, laughing and talking in clusters. The kids ran from room to room, giddy with excitement and hunger.

I slipped into the kitchen to watch the last-minute preparations. Dorothea carefully pulled open the oven, basting the turkey to a deep golden brown, while the other women rushed around her, stirring pots on the stove, grabbing copper and terra cotta bowls off the shelves to fill with mashed potatoes, sweet potatoes, creamed onions, salad, and hot rolls. Back and forth they ran, carrying the heavy bowls and platters to the table.

"Ready!" cried Dorothea victoriously when everything was done, and Dan came in with two big oven mitts to carry the turkey to the table.

We didn't all fit in the dining room, so two old ship's tables that ran the length of the living room were set out, covered with white tablecloths, edged around by old, creaking wooden benches. While Paul carved the turkey, we gathered, fidgeting, laughing, and talking, to sit at the table.

I knew it was still a long, long time till we'd eat, and the strong, delicious smells of the food made waiting feel impossible. Someone had set the pitcher of gravy in front of my place, and a rich, meaty smell came steaming up from inside.

Finally Paul finished carving, laid aside his knife, and wiped his hands on a dishtowel. Dorothea handed him some papers.

Quietness spread from the head of the long table down to the end under the windows. There was a pause, a stillness like the moment before the curtain goes up in the theater. Paul was going to take us back, back to first decree of Thanksgiving in America, as starvation came creeping in on the new settlers from Europe.

"We'll begin," said Paul, "with the Charleston records, 1630." He stood tall and read in a clear, strong voice. Romantic and idealistic in his love of democracy, he went on to read Abraham Lincoln's entire Thanksgiving Proclamation from October 3, 1863.

My attention wandered, and I started swinging my leg back and forth under the table, kicking my sister Meg, who was sitting next to me. Meg kicked me right back, hard, making me jump.

I looked up to see Dorothea staring at us, a look of disapproval on her face. Quickly, I turned back to Paul, giving him my full, wholehearted attention, just as he finished the proclamation.

Listening to the Thanksgiving Proclamation, 1962 (Photograph by Ron Partridge)

"'Grace for a Pagan,'" Paul announced next. "By Maynard Dixon."

"Who's Maynard Dixon?" whispered Meg.

"He's dead," I whispered back. "He used to paint pictures."

"Lord of the Universe," Paul began. "Inscrutable power, under thy Dominion we live. We pray, therefore, that this food be consecrated to our use, that we may fulfill our lives in kindness and forbearance, in honesty and justice within thy law. Amen."

Murmured amens echoed around the table from the adults. "Serve the turkey, Paul!" cried Dorothea, rushing forward to pass the plates. The blue bowl full of mashed potatoes passed hand to hand down to where I sat, then the cranberry relish, the platter heaped with turkey, the creamed onions and rolls.

When my plate was covered with food, I reached for the gravy pitcher and raised it with both hands, wobbling and heavy.

Dorothea's voice carried over the hubbub. "Carefully, Bitsie," she said. "Carefully."

And carefully I poured the gravy.

Thankful, joyful, and hungry, we ate.

Dorothea at Dinner, 1961 (Photograph by Ron Partridge)

BIBLIOGRAPHIC NOTE

"The words that come direct from the people are the greatest."

The best sources for this biography were those in the words of Dorothea herself. These include an oral history, *The Making of a Documentary Photographer*, by Suzanne Riess (Berkeley: Regional History Office, Bancroft Library, University of California, 1968); and an interview by Richard K. Doud (transcript in the Archives of American Art, Smithsonian Institution, 1964). A film crew from KQED in San Francisco made two films, *Closer for Me*, and *Under the Trees*, for National Educational Television. They often left a microphone running, taping Dorothea as she put together her MOMA show from 1963 to 1965. These tapes are held by the Dorothea Lange Collection in the Oakland Museum of California. Also useful were my sister Meg Partridge's film, *Dorothea Lange: A Visual Life* (Pacific Pictures, 1993); and Dorothea's letters and journals. Some quotations from these sources were rambling, so to streamline them, I sometimes left out words without adding ellipses. All the quotations following chapter titles are Dorothea's own words.

People close to Dorothea were generous in sharing their memories. These include her two sons, John and Dan Dixon; her daughter-in-law Helen Dixon; and two of her assistants, Christina Gardner and my father Ron Partridge. I also relied heavily on Suzanne Riess's oral history of Dorothea's second husband, *Paul Schuster Taylor, California Social Scientist* (Berkeley: Regional History Office, Bancroft Library, University of California, 1973).

For an overview of Dorothea's life, I turned to the excellent biography by Milton Meltzer, *Dorothea Lange: A Photographer's Life* (New York: Farrar, Straus & Giroux, 1978).

Additional sources used for individual chapters include:

Foreword
NAT HERZ, "Dorothea Lange in Perspective," *Infinity* 12 (April 1963).
DOROTHEA LANGE, "The Assignment I'll Never Forget: Migrant Mother," *Popular Photography* 46 (February 1961).
PAUL S. TAYLOR, "Again the Covered Wagon," *Survey Graphic Magazine*, July 1935.
Unpublished e-mail from Troy Owens, one of the migrant mother's sons, to Paul Stein March 1998.

Chapter 2
THERESE THAU HEYMAN, *Celebrating a Collection: The Work of Dorothea Lange* (Oakland: Oakland Museum, 1978).
OSCAR LEWIS, *Bay Window Bohemia* (Garden City, N.Y.: Doubleday and Co., 1956).

118

Chapter 3
The Thunderbird Remembered: Maynard Dixon, the Man and the Artist. (Seattle: Gene Autry Western Heritage Museum Publication in association with the University of Washington Press, 1994).

Chapter 5
KEITH DAVIS, *The Photographs of Dorothea Lange* (Kansas City: Hallmark Cards, 1995).

JERRY STANLEY, *Children of the Dust Bowl: The True Story of the School at Weedpatch Camp* (New York: Crown Publishers, 1992).

PAUL TAYLOR, with photographs by Dorothea Lange, *American Exodus: A Record of Human Erosion* (New York: Reynal and Hitchcock, 1939).

Chapters 6, 7, and 8
KARIN OHRN, *Dorothea Lange and the Documentary Tradition* (Baton Rouge: Louisiana State University Press, 1980).

JOHN STEINBECK AND CHARLES WOLLENBURG, *The Harvest Gypsies: On the Road to the Grapes of Wrath* (Berkeley: Heyday Press, 1996).

Chapter 9
The Auburn Journal Republican, Jan. 18, 1945

MAISIE CONRAT AND RICHARD CONRAT, *Executive Order 9066: The Internment of 110,000 Japanese Americans* (Los Angeles: California State Historical Society, 1972)

ROGER DANIELS, *Prisoners Without Trial: Japanese Americans in World War II* (New York: Hill and Wang, 1993).

JERRY STANLEY, *I Am an American: A True Story of Japanese Internment* (New York: Crown Publishers, 1994).

Chapter 10
PENNY COLMAN, *Rosie the Riveter: Women Working on the Homefront in World War II* (New York: Crown Publishers, 1995)

CHARLES WOLLENBURG, *Photographing the Second Gold Rush: Dorothea Lange and the East Bay at War* (Berkeley: Heydey Books, 1995).

Chapter 11
DANIEL DIXON, "Dorothea Lange," *Modern Photography* 16:12 (December 1952).

Chapter 12
Letter from Dorothea to Beaumont Newhall, written when she knew she had incurable cancer, September 15, 1964.

Letter from Paul Taylor to the family members after Dorothea's death, recounting her last moments, 1965.

INDEX

Titles of photographs appear in *italics*.

Adams, Ansel, 47, 91

African-Americans, 91, 93

Agribusiness, 65-73

Alstrom, Florence "Fronsie," 13, 14, 20, 28

"America's Many Faces," 100

Andrew, Berkeley, 1959, 108

Bad Trouble over the Weekend, 1964, 110

Barrymore, John, 17

Bitsie and Dorothea, 1961, 112

"Bitter Years, The," 100

"Bloody Thursday," 45

Bohemians, 20-25, 31

Boumphrey, Jack, 22

Bound for California, Oklahoma, 1938, 53

Bourke-White, Margaret, 55

Bowery, 13, 40

Bowery, early 1900s, 14

Boy in Ecuador, 1960, 103

Child of a Migratory Worker, San Joaquin Valley, California, 1936, 61

Children, photographs of, 5

Children at Raphael Weill Public School Before the Evacuation, San Francisco, 1942, 83

Children of Carrot Pickers, California, 1937, 66

Children Reading, Steep Ravine, 1961, 109

Citizens' Anti-Japanese League, 89

Civilian Conservation Corps (CCC), 43-44

Collins, Tom, 69-70

Columbia University, 18-19

Consie with Maynard's Horse, ca. 1920, 29

Cunningham, Imogen, 21, 22, 27, 47, 48

Crystal Palace Plunge, 42

Dixon, Andrew, 100, 114

Dixon, Consie, 29, 32

Dixon, Daniel, 31, 40, 48, 57, 111, 114; boarded out, 35-37, 42, 44, 50, 75; as rebel, 73, 79, 92, 97, 98; as writer, 98, 99, 101

Dixon, Gregor, 99, 114

Dixon, Helen, 99-100, 111, 114

Dixon, John, 31, 40, 57, 73, 111, 114; boarded out, 35-37, 42, 44, 50, 75; family of, 99-100

Dixon, Leslie, 114

Dixon, Lisa, 114

Dixon, Maynard, 117; death of, 95; described, 24-25, 27; ill health of, 32, 35; marriage to Dorothea, 27-28; painting exhibitions of, 31, 33-35; relationship with wife, 32, 35-37, 40-43, 53, 56

Dixon, Mia, 114

Dorothea, 1920s, 16

Dorothea, Berkeley, 1936, vi

Dorothea and Martin, 1905, 6

Dorothea and Paul, Utah, 1953, 96

Dorothea and Paul Taylor, 1939, 46

Dorothea at Dinner, 1961, 117

Dorothea Basting the Turkey, 1962, 114

Dorothea Being Shown How to Tie on a Potato Sack, 1937, 64

Dorothea Digging Potatoes, 1937, 64

Dorothea in New Jersey, ca. 1947, 90

Dorothea in the Field, 1938, 54

Dorothea in the Kitchen, 1936, 26

Dorothea Lange, 1934, 38

Dorothea Lange Photographing the Japanese-American Evacuation, 1942, 80

Dorothea with Zeiss Jewel Camera, 1937, 74

Dust bowl, 52, 65

Episcopal Home for Working Girls, 20

Evans, Walker, 55

Fallen Leaf Lake, 47-48

Fallen Leaf Lake with the Partridge Boys, 1934, 47

"Family of Man, The," 100

Family on Street Corner, Ecuador, 1960, 102

Family on the Road, San Joaquin Valley, California, 1935, 51

Farm Security Administration (FSA), 55, 65, 68-73, 78

Father and Son on a Tractor, Texas, 1938, 76

Federal Emergency Relief Administration (FERA), 44, 53

Firstborn, 1952, 99

Fischer, Dorothea, 8

Fortune magazine, 91
442 Regimental Combat
    Team, 89
FSA Camp for Migrant Workers,
    Arvin, California, 1936, 68

Garbo, Greta, 17
Gardner, Chrissie, 84, 86
Garst, Jonathan, 79
General Strike (Policeman), San
    Francisco, 1934, 45
Genthe, Arnold, 17-18
Gertrude Clausen, Holding Nancy,
    studio portrait, 1932, 23
Getting on Evacuation Bus,
    Centerville, California, 1942,
    86
Girl Carrying Full Cotton Sack,
    California, 1936, 72
Girls of Lincoln Bench School,
    Oregon, 1939, 67
Grandmother Sophie, 10
Grapes of Wrath, The
    (Steinbeck), 72-73
Great Depression, 1-5, 32, 39-79

Helen and Andrew, 1955, 100
High School Boys Before
    Evacuation, San Francisco,
    1942, 82
Hitler, Adolf, 79, 81, 91
Hoboken, New Jersey, 7-8, 11,
    20
Homeless Boy and Cat at a
    CCC Camp, California, ca.
    1934, 43
Hop Harvesting, Oregon, 1939, 71
Hopi Man, 1920s, 35

Japanese American internment,
    81-89
Jefferson, Thomas, 48
Jews, 12-13

Kinnikinnick, 27, 32

Kipling, Rudyard, 20
Korean Child, 1958, 104
Lange, Dorothea: abandonment
    by father, 10, 22; cameras
    of, 59, 98; childhood of, 7-
    15; "cloak of invisibility," 13;
    darkroom of, 19-20; death
    of, 110-11; desire to be a
    photographer, 15, 17-19; as
    "Dictator Dot," 56-57, 73;
    first husband of, *see* Dixon,
    Maynard; freedom and, 31;
    given name of, 8, 22; ill
    health of, 73, 94-95, 97-98,
    101, 105, 107, 110-11; as
    mother, 31-37, 79, 110;
    mother and, 8, 10-15; as
    photographer of people, 48;
    plight of women and, 31-35;
    second husband of, *see*
    Taylor, Paul; show at MOMA,
    107-11; as stepmother, 29,
    56-57; Stryker and, 78-79;
    studio of, 22, 24, 56; as
    teacher, 15, 17, 19; temper
    of, 29; Thanksgiving dinner
    with, 113-17; trips abroad,
    101, 105, 107; as victim of
    polio, 8, 22, 43, 59, 100
Lange, Sophie, 10-11, 13
Lee, Russell, 55
Life magazine, 101
Lincoln, Abraham, 115
Listening to the Thanksgiving
    Proclamation, 1962, 116
Lower East Side, 11-13
Lower East Side of Manhattan,
    early 1900s, 12
Lunch Break, Richmond Shipyards,
    California, 1943, 95
Lyde Wall, Northern California,
    1944, 97

Man Beside Wheelbarrow, San
    Francisco, 1934, 42

Manzanar, 87-88
Manzanar Relocation Center,
    1942, 87
Maynard and Boys, End of the
    Visit, ca. 1934, 36
Maynard and Dan Painting, early
    1930s, 33
Maynard and John at Alta, 1929, 30
Maynard Dixon at His Easel, ca.
    1920, 28
Midsummer Night's Dream, A
    (Shakespeare), 9-10
Migrant farm workers, 1-5, 50-
    73; camps for, 68-73; children
    of, 63, 66-67; conditions
    faced by, 59-63
Migrant Mother (1), Nipomo,
    California, 1936, 2
Migrant Mother (2), Nipomo,
    California, 1936, 3
Migrant Mother (4), Nipomo,
    California, 1936, 4
Mochida Family Awaiting
    Evacuation Bus, 1942, 85
Mother's Day Daisies, 1934, 32
Mrs. Kahn and Child, San Francisco,
    studio portrait, 1928, 24
Museum of Modern Art
    (MOMA), 107-10
My Childhood Home, 1940s, 11
My Mother the "Wuz," 1920s, 9

New York Training School for
    Teachers, 17, 19
Nikkei, 81-89
Nutzhorn, Henry, 7-10, 22
Nutzhorn, Joan, 7-15
Nutzhorn, Martin, 8, 13, 32, 92

Oklahoma Child with Cotton
    Sack Ready to Go into the
    Field, 7 A.M., California,
    1936, 70
One of the Wandering Homeless
    Boys, ca. 1934, 44

Pacific Coast Committee for American Principles and Fair Play, 89

Partridge, Bitsie, 113-17

Partridge, Meg, 115, 117

Partridge, Pad, 47

Partridge, Roi, 20-21, 22, 28, 31, 47

Partridge, Ron, 31, 47, 63, 97; as photographer, vi, 45, 57-59, 84, 113

Paul Carrying Lisa, Steep Ravine, 1962, 109

People Living in Miserable Poverty, Shacktown, Oklahoma, 1936, 60

Pickford, Mary, 17

Portrait Photograph of Arnold Genthe Taken Outdoors, 18

Preparing for Evacuation, Sacramento Country, California, May 1942, 84

Public School 62, 13

Richmond School Children—Every Hand Up Signifies a Child Not Born in California, 1942, 94

Roi Partridge, San Francisco, 1925, 21

Ron Partridge, 1939, 57

Ron Partridge Photographing at Hooverville, 1939, 58

Roosevelt, Franklin D., 43-45, 81, 82, 83

Roosevelt, Teddy, 17

Ross Taylor, Driven and Angry, 1935, 56

Rothstein, Arthur, 55

San Francisco, 20-25, 44-45

San Francisco News, 5, 68

Schoolroom, Egypt, 1963, 102

"Self-Help Beats Charity," 48

Shafter Camp, 69-70

Shahn, Ben, 55

Shakespeare, William, 9-10

Sharecroppers, 75-79

Shipyards, 91-95

Shipyard Workers Children at Window, Richmond, California, 1943, 93

Sick Migrant Child, Washington, 1939, 62

Sixth Grade Students Studying at the Volunteer Elementary School, Manzanar, 1942, 88

South, the, 75-79

Southwest, ca. 1930, 34

Starving pea pickers, 1-6

State Emergency Relief Administration (SERA), 50, 52-53

Steep Ravine, 101, 111

Steinbeck, John, 70, 72-73

Strand, Paul, 35

Stryker, Roy, 55-56, 65, 69, 73, 77-79

Supreme Court, U.S., 89

Szarkowski, John, 107, 111

Taft, William Howard, 17

Tanforan, 86-87

Taos, New Mexico, 32-35

Taylor, Katherine, 56-57, 73, 99

Taylor, Margot, 56-57, 73, 99

Taylor, Paul, 92, 114, 117; described, 48; Dorothea's illness and, 101, 105, 107, 110-11; marriage to Dorothea, 53, 56, 89, 95; SERA and, 50, 52-53, 68, 78-79

Taylor, Ross, 56-57, 73, 99; family of, 114

Taylor-Lange reports, 52-53, 55

"Their Blood Is Strong," 72

Thirteen-Year-Old Sharecropper Cultivating a Field, Georgia, 1937, 77

Tom Collins and Migrant Family, Shafter, California, 1936, 69

Unemployed Exchange Association (UXA), 48-50

Unemployment Exchange Association (UXA), Oroville, California, 1934, 49

Wadleigh High School for Girls, 14-15

Wall, Lyde, 97-98

War Relocation Authority (WRA), 83

Waterboy, Mississippi Delta, 1938, 79

Welder, Richmond Shipyards, California, 1943, 92

Western Union, 20

White, Clarence, 18-19

White Angel bread line, 39-40

White Angel Bread Line, San Francisco, 1933, 41

Wilder, Richmond Shipyards, California, 1943, 42

Wilson, Woodrow, 17

Wilson family, 29, 32

Working on the MOMA Show, 1964, 106

World War II, 79, 81; Bay Area shipyards during, 91-95; internment of Japanese during, 81-89

Young Sharecropper and His First Child, North Carolina, 1939, 78